SECULARISM CONFRONTS ISLAM

SECULARISM
CONFRONTS
ISLAM

OLIVIER ROY

TRANSLATED BY GEORGE HOLOCH

COLUMBIA UNIVERSITY PRESS  NEW YORK

Ouvrage publié avec le soutien du Centre national du livre–ministère français chargé de la culture. / Work published with the support of the National Book Center–French Ministry of Culture.

Columbia University Press
Publishers Since 1893
New York Chichester, West Sussex

Library of Congress Cataloging-in-Publication Data
Roy, Olivier, 1949–
[Laïcité face à l'islam. English]
Secularism confronts Islam / Olivier Roy ; translated by George Holoch.
p. cm.
Includes bibliographical references and index.
ISBN-13: 978-0-231-14102-4 (cloth : alk. paper)
ISBN-13: 978-0-231-51179-7 (electronic)
1. Islam—France. 2. Islam and secularism—France. 3. Islam and state—France. 4. Laicism—France. 5. Fundamentalism—France. I. Title.

BP65.F8R6913   2007
322'.10944—dc22   2007001748

∞

Columbia University Press books are printed on permanent and durable acid-free paper.
Printed in the United States of America
c 10 9 8 7 6 5 4 3 2

CONTENTS

PREFACE

Islam's encounter with the West is as old as Islam itself. The first Muslim minorities living under Western Christian domination date back to the eleventh century (in Sicily). Yet the second half of the twentieth century witnessed a distinctively new phenomenon: the massive, voluntary settlement in Western societies of millions of Muslims coming from Muslim societies across the Middle East, the Indian subcontinent, Turkey, Africa, and Southeast Asia. The West has also witnessed the development of an indigenous trend of religious conversion (as in the case of the Nation of Islam). And yet, while a Muslim population has definitively taken root in the West, the question of its integration remains open, especially in western Europe, where there is an overlap between Islam and work-driven immigration—an overlap that is not to be found in the United States. Socioeconomic problems, cultural issues, and political tensions related to terrorism or the conflicts in the Middle East converge around the question: Is Islam compatible with the West? Of course, this question rests on an essentialist worldview, according to which there is *one* Islam, on the one hand, and *one*

Western world, on the other hand. From that perspective, the West is allegedly defined by a set of values (freedom of expression, democracy, separation of church and state, human rights, and, especially, women's rights). But a problem immediately arises: Are these Christian values? Is the opposition between Islam and the West derived from the fact that the West is Christian? Or is it rather because the West is secularized and no longer locates religion at the heart of its self-definition? Is it Christianity or secularism that makes the West so distinct?

The relation between secularism and Christianity is complex. Either one defines the West in Christian terms, or one defines it in reference to the philosophy of the Enlightenment, human rights, and democracy that developed against the Catholic Church, through first the Protestant Reformation, then the Enlightenment, and finally a secular and democratic ideal. If the Catholic Church has always fought secularism and the separation of church and state (at least until the beginning of the twentieth century), Protestantism has played a more complex role by defending a sort of religious civil society in which the separation of church and state is seen as a necessary condition for a genuine religious revival. Secularization therefore proceeds differently in Catholic and Protestant societies— against faith in the former, along with faith in the latter—to such an extent that it is difficult to talk about *the* West.

Contemporary Western societies, however, are, in fact, secularized, either because the separation of church and state is a constitutional principle (the United States), because civil society no longer defines itself through faith and religious practice (the United Kingdom, Germany, the Scandinavian countries), or because these two forms of secularism converge and reinforce each other, thus giving birth to what the French call *laïcité*. And yet when one opposes the West and Islam, it is by putting forward the Christian origins of Western culture or, on the contrary, by emphasizing its secularism. In other words, when we question Islam's capacity to become "Westernized," we are referring to two different forms of Westernization: Christianization and secularization. Of course, things are more complex, and it would be easy to show that Western secularism actually has a Christian origin—as I do in this book. But it is interesting to see that the critique of Islam is today a rallying point for two intellectual families that have been opposed to each other so far: those who think that the West is first and foremost Christian (and who, not that long ago, considered that the Jews could hardly be assimilated) and those who think that the West is primarily secular and democratic. In other words, the Christian Right and the secular Left are today united in their criticism of Islam.

But if Christianity has been able to recast itself as one religion among others in a secular space, why would this be impossible for Islam? Two arguments are usually summoned to make this case: the first is theological and says that the separation between religion and politics is foreign to Islam; the second is cultural and posits that Islam is more than a religion: it is a culture. Both arguments will be addressed in this book. But this theoretical debate, which thrives on op-ed pieces and talk shows, is increasingly solved in the practice of Muslims themselves. The experience of everyday life as a minority brings Muslims to develop practices, compromises, and considerations meant to cope with a secularism that imposes itself on them. This does not mean that Islam has never experienced secularism but only that, with the exception of a few isolated thinkers, it never felt the need to think about it. Today, both life conditions in the West and the domination of the Western model through the process of globalization compel many Muslims to relate explicitly to this form of secularism, somewhat urgently and under the pressure of political events. This reflection spans a very wide intellectual spectrum that goes from what I call neofundamentalism to liberal positions, proceeding through all kinds of more or less enlightened conservatism.[1]

Unfortunately, the paradigms and models mobilized in the Western debate over Islam hardly reflect the real practices of Muslims. While the political debate over the potential danger allegedly represented by Muslims is more or less inspired by the intellectual debate about the "clash of civilizations," the help of sociology (that is, the concrete analysis of Muslim practices) is hardly sought—even though sociology is at pains to grasp the concrete forms of religiosity that characterize the practice of Islam within immigrant communities. One must therefore abandon the current models in order to understand how it is possible to practice one's faith as a Muslim in a secularized Western context. And one quickly realizes then that Muslims tend to find themselves in a position that is closer to that of the born-again Christians or the Haredi Jews than to the position of a stranger.

So far, the West has managed its Muslim population by mobilizing two models: multiculturalism, usually associated with English-speaking countries (the United Kingdom, the United States, Canada) and northern Europe, and the assimilationist model, specific to France. Multiculturalism supposes that Islam as a religion is embedded in a distinct culture that maintains itself from one generation to the next. One can be a good citizen and at the same time identify primarily with a culture that is not the dominant one. In other words, the citizen's relation to the nation can be mediated by a communitarian sense of belonging. In the assimilationist model (the official term is "integration"), access to citizenship (which turns out to be relatively easy) means that individual cultural backgrounds are erased and overridden by a political community, the nation, that ignores all intermediary communitarian attachments (whether based on race or on ethnic or religious identities), which are then removed to the private sphere. As was declared in the French National Assembly during the vote that granted full citizenship to French Jews in 1791: "They must be granted everything as individuals and nothing as a nation" (in the sense of community). Nothing could be more opposed than the multicultural and assimilationist models: the French consider Anglo-Saxon multiculturalism either as the destruction of national unity or as an instrument of ghettoization, while assimilationism is perceived abroad as the expression of an authoritarian, centralized state that refuses to recognize minority rights, when it does not infringe on human rights.

Yet the recent tensions that have troubled Western societies since September 11 show that both these models are in crisis. In France, many young Muslims complain that theirs is a second-class citizenship and that they are still the victims of racism, while they are integrated in terms of language and education and accept *laïcité*. Moreover, also in France, young born-again Muslims demand to be recognized as believers in the public space (by wearing a veil, if they are girls). At the same time, the increasing radicalization of a fraction of Muslim youth in the United Kingdom and in the Netherlands has led to a shift in public opinion in these countries, whereby the multicultural model is called into question and accused of encouraging "separatism."

As a matter of fact, both multiculturalism and assimilationism are in crisis for similar reasons: both posit the existence of an intrinsic link between religion and culture. Keeping one's religion also means keeping one's culture. Multiculturalism therefore implies that religion remains embedded in a stable cultural background, and assimiliationism implies that integration, by definition, leads to the secularization of beliefs and behaviors, since all cultural backgrounds disappear. But the problem is that today's religious revival—whether under fundamentalist or spiritualistic forms—develops by decoupling itself from any cultural reference. It thrives on the loss of cultural identity: the young radicals are indeed perfectly "Westernized." Among the born-again and the converts (numerous young women who want to wear the veil belong to these categories), Islam is seen not as a cultural relic but as a religion that is universal and global and reaches beyond specific cultures, just like evangelicalism or Pentecostalism. And this loss of cultural identity is the condition both for integration and for new forms of fundamentalism.[2] Whether Muslim, Christian, or Jewish, religious revivalism raises the question of the place of religion in the public sphere. The debates about prayers in school, the display of the Ten Commandments in courthouses, or the creation of an *eruv* following the request of Haredi Jews to "privatize" public space on Shabbat show that the recasting of the relation between the religious and the public sphere is not specific to Islam.[3]

Why, then, pay so much attention to French *laïcité*, which until now seemed to be an exception? There is today a convergence of the various debates taking place in Western countries: tellingly, they focus on the veil worn by some Muslim women (prohibition of the headscarf in French high schools, increasingly vocal critique of the burka—that is, of the integral veil—in the United Kingdom and in the Netherlands). The real issue here is indeed the articulation of religious identity within the public sphere and therefore the question of secularism. This debate started in France in 1989 and was continued in the United Kingdom in 2006, following the declarations against the burka made by the leader of the House of Commons, Jack Straw. Is France an exception, or does it represent a real alternative to multiculturalism? Here lies the interest of studying the French model. From a historical point of view, there is indeed a French exception: France may be the only democracy that has fought religion in order to impose a state-enforced secularism. In France, *laïcité* is an exacerbated, politicized, and ideological form of Western secularism that has developed on two levels:

1. A very strict separation of church and state, against the backdrop of a political conflict between the state and the Catholic Church that resulted in a law regulating very strictly the presence of religion in the public sphere (1905). This is what I call legal *laïcité*.

2. An ideological and philosophical interpretation of *laïcité* that claims to provide a value system common to all citizens by expelling religion into the private sphere. I call this ideological *laïcité*: today, it leads the majority of the secular Left to strike an alliance with the Christian Right against Islam.

Laïcité therefore defines national cohesion by asserting a purely political identity that confines to the private sphere any specific religious or cultural identities. Outside France, this very offensive and militant *laïcité* is perceived as excessive, and even undemocratic, since it violates individual freedom. It is regularly denounced in the annual report of the State Department on religious freedom in the world (not only because of the prohibition of the Muslim veil but also because of the restrictions placed on the activities of sects such as Jehovah's Witnesses and the Scientologists).[4]

Yet, over a short period of time, the initial hostility of European multiculturalist countries toward the French model has turned into a renewed interest: What if the French were right? A sizable number of countries that have embraced multiculturalism so far are about to restrict the wearing of the Islamic veil (the Netherlands, the United Kingdom, Belgium, Germany). This interest in *laïcité* is primarily negative: it stems from the crisis (from the death, I would even argue) of multiculturalism. If the multicultural model has failed, then one should look at the alternative represented by the French model. But is French *laïcité* a solution? How does it work? Isn't it too specific to the French context? How can one imagine both the national cohesion of Western societies and the development, beyond specific cultures, of "faith communities" based on individual and voluntary choices, which, however, put forward their specific agendas? Communitarianism and individualism go hand in hand in these faith communities. The redefinition of the relations between religion and politics is a new challenge for the West, and not only because of Islam. Islam is a mirror in which the West projects its own identity crisis. We live in a postculturalist society, and this postculturalism is the very foundation of the contemporary religious revival.

Managing these new forms of religiosity is a challenge for the West as a whole. It is also a task to which this book intends to contribute, by drawing the lessons from the French debate, but only to resituate it in the general context of the relations between Islam and the West.

SECULARISM CONFRONTS ISLAM

INTRODUCTION
Laïcité and the Identity of France

The question of *laïcité* in France has recently given rise to violent polemics going well beyond intellectual debate into the realm of personalities.[1] The law on the veil and the deportation of imams were accompanied by hundreds of editorials and op-ed pieces in the press and a significant number of best-selling books in which the denunciation of fundamentalism soon shifted into a systematic attack on Muslims and Islam in general: the so-called Islamic threat was on the covers of all the magazines.[2] This polemical violence, which has recently been given the name "Islamophobia" and which comes from very diverse political contexts,[3] clearly demonstrates that the problem of Islam in France today is practically an existential one: Islam seems to call into question the very identity of the country, or at least the nature of its institutions. People mobilize for the defense of "republican values" and "*laïcité*."

But why has the debate over French identity focused on Islam? Militant *laïcité* is an old story; it has been at war against private Catholic education at least since 1905 (and there are still no real private Muslim schools). Christian sects and evangelical denomi-

1

nations of every stripe have proliferated far beyond Catholic precincts. Is Islam such a threat, or has French identity reached such a crisis point that a few hundred veiled girls and bearded preachers can overwhelm it? The debate has to be situated in the context of the history of French *laïcité*, which found its clearest expression in the 1905 law on the separation of church and state. At the time, the enemy was the Catholic Church (*"clericalism, that's the enemy!"*), and Islam has now taken the place of Catholicism. But the real question is whether this represents a continuity or a break. In the end, is the debate about Islam concerned with the place of religion in French society, or, despite the apparent continuity, is Islam today seen as a different religion, the bearer of a specific threat? In that case, is this due to the specific character of Muslim theology or, more prosaically, to the fact that Islam is the religion of immigrants, which automatically projects onto France the shadow of conflicts in the Middle East? All of that is obviously mixed together, inevitably, to the extent that Islam in the West is demographically the result of recent, voluntary, and massive immigration from Muslim countries. Demonstrating that there is an old tradition of Muslim presence and contacts with Islam would do little to change the current perception of the problem. But if it is immigration or the Middle East that is the source of difficulty, then that has to be said clearly, and we can stop the endless stream of quotations from the Koran. And if it is only Islam that is at issue, then we have to stop thinking about Islam from the perspective of the *banlieue* and the *banlieue* from the perspective of Islam.[4]

But the question goes much further than that. The campaign of Islamophobia we are witnessing today is involved in the reshaping of the French political and intellectual landscape, for we find in it several elements that until now have not gone together. Obviously very hostile to the presence both of immigrants and of Islam are those who think that the Christian heritage is part of French and European identity and thus that Islam cannot be integrated into it, even in a secular form (Oriana Fallaci, Alain Besançon, Alexandre

2

Del Valle). This is the traditional position of the Christian Right and of the extreme Right (the latter often adding an ethnic or even a racist dimension, which is blatant in Oriana Fallaci's book). But to this hostility toward Islam, which may be called traditional, has been added today that of circles claiming to represent the republic and *laïcité*, combating not immigrants but what they perceive as a fundamentalism more threatening than its Christian counterpart (this is the tenor of attacks launched against Tariq Ramadan by writers like Caroline Fourest). In this campaign, conducted primarily by figures on the Left, two lines can be discerned: the pessimists, for whom there is no secular Islam, and the optimists, who, on the contrary, want to foster, or even bring into being, an Islam that would be liberal, secular, and truly French. Many politicians on the Left have adopted this stance (Didier Motchane, Manuel Valls). But for some republicans, who have broken with the Left they have long criticized for its fascination with the Third World (Pierre-André Taguieff, Alain Finkielkraut), the problem lies not only with fundamentalism but with its relationship to Third Worldism, anti-Zionism, and even, in their view, anti-Semitism and the extreme Right (what they call the red-green-brown alliance): for them, the *banlieues* identify with the Palestinians, and communitarianism reflects a global conflict. They denounce the Economic and Social Forum for having invited Ramadan to attend and the notorious conference against racism held by the United Nations in Durban in 2001 for having accused Israel of racism. In this case, the problem is not so much Islam itself as the Arabic—and hence presumably pro-Palestinian and anti-Israeli—component of immigration. In opposition, a part of the Left and the extreme Left has remained faithful to the defense of the Third World and the oppressed, emphasizing the social and neocolonial aspects of current conflicts (Alain Gresh, François Burgat): they obviously reject any assimilation to the extreme Right and see the conflict as one between North and South, developed countries and the Third World, the excluded and the privileged. The debates that stirred the conference sponsored by the Mouvement contre le racisme et pour l'amitié entre les peuples (Movement Against Racism and for Friendship Among Peoples) in December 2004 clearly illustrate the question: Should the struggle against Islamophobia be mentioned in the context of the struggle against racism? Is Islam an element of ethnic and cultural identity, or is it only a religion? The denunciation of Muslim fundamentalism thus masks other targets and other stakes. The label of "fundamentalism," which is very useful for polemics, is applied from the outside. When Muslims are called on to adopt a reformed and liberal Islam, they are expected to situate themselves in relation to an analytical framework that has been prepared for them without asking questions about the meaning of their practices and the nature of choices involving their identity. But very clearly, everything connected to an open (but not necessarily ostentatious) affirmation of Islam is considered the harbinger of a dangerous fundamentalism.

We are thus witnessing a blurring of traditional divisions and a holy secular alliance between currents that opposed each other in the past. In the early twentieth century, those who saw Europe as a Christian land rejected the stateless Jews and also opposed republican *laïcité*.[5] These Christian-identity advocates reject Islam but, in their opposition to homosexual marriage and their criticisms of what they call the excesses of feminism, find themselves in agreement with Muslim fundamentalists against a liberal Left that defends sexual minorities but has now called into question its relationship to religious minorities. Today, a segment of the secular Left that in the 1980s defended the rights of immigrants against the Front National is indignant that the children of those immigrants display a Muslim identity and sometimes holds, despite itself, positions that were those of the Front National, but with the clear conscience of those who still see themselves as antiracist.[6] Religious practices associated with an immigrant culture were tolerated (the slaughter of a sheep outside an apartment building for the end of Ramadan) but become unbearable when they take their place definitively on the stage of French society as the affirmation of a faith detached from any foreign culture (the *hallal* supermarket in Evry forced to close under pressure). The universalism of the Left has shattered against Islam. Conversely, another segment of the Left attacks Islamophobia and defends the right to wear the veil in school (the association Écoles pour tous et toutes [Schools for All] and a minority of feminists such as Françoise Gaspard), a defense, by the way, much more tied to individual rights than to the praise of multiculturalism, which remains, whatever its detractors may claim, absent from the French scene. But it must be noted that more and more former assimilationists on the Left now find themselves adopting very right-wing positions.[7] As for those who see in Islamo-progressivism a new convergence between extreme Left and extreme Right and consider anti-Zionism as an expression of anti-Semitism, they have difficulty defending hard-line *laïcité* at a time when orthodox religious communitarianism is growing in France and Israeli society is debating the relationship among citizenship, ethnicity, and religion.[8] In every case, those for whom the underlying problem has always been immigration—that is, the ethnic (if not racial) question—have now joined those for whom the central question is religion: the theme (and the denunciation) of communitarianization is what unites the two currents. Immigration and the place of Islam are linked, even though the link will gradually be loosened in reality, as new generations, the descendants of immigrants, no longer see themselves as the custodians of a native culture.

Another element arises from the fact that in France Muslims have begun to speak as Muslims. The immigrant of the 1970s was silent: others spoke for him. The young *beurs* of the 1980s,[9] when they went outside their *banlieues*, laid claim to the prevailing language of integration instead of defending a difference, except for skin color: they were above all antiracist, that is, against any insignia of otherness; they rejected any communitarianism and made no reference to Islam. This was the very nature of the march of the *beurs* in 1983, and it remains the line of the association SOS-Racisme, which came out of the 1983 movement but is now disconnected from the *banlieues*. What appeared later, in the 1990s, was a structured Islamic discourse embodied by two figures: the bearded Salafist preacher, in a white djellaba and with a heavy accent, come from the East to haunt the *banlieues* that had been transformed into forbidden zones, and the impeccably dressed intellectual speaking perfect French, who spoke in praise of a fundamental difference, a belief that displayed itself without complexes. And if we are to judge by recent publications, it is the latter figure, embodied by Tariq Ramadan, who has created the greatest anxiety. The cliché of dual language for which Tariq Ramadan is constantly criticized is obviously aimed at assimilating the speech of the second figure to the preaching of the first and at denying everything that is a matter of the elaboration and transformation of a discourse that is, to be sure, Salafist in origin.[10] But this work on Salafist discourse, which is Ramadan's contribution, is paid no heed. And yet it raises a basic question: that of the sudden emergence in all Western monotheistic religions of new forms of religiosity, all of them communitarian (but of a purely religious community), exclusive (a clear dividing line separates the saved from the damned), and inclusive (all aspects of life must be placed by the believer under the aegis of religion). The phenomenon of sects is troubling to French society, and the temptation to legislate against them is as strong as in the case of Islam. Misgivings about Islam are consistent with suspicion of religions, accentuated by the appearance of new communities of believers who do not feel bound by the compromises laboriously developed over the past century between *cathos* and *laïques*. At the same time, it is not adequate to compare Muslim religious revivalism with Protestant evangelical movements or the Jehovah's Witnesses. Because of immigration and the situation in the Middle East, there is a much stronger political dimension in the question of Islam. Finally, as always, the most active participants in the debate are the militants: the great mass of moderates, Muslims who have developed their personal *laïcité* and who are well established in French society, do not participate in the debate, until the day, of course, when they have thrown in their faces their membership in a group that they have never experienced as conflictual or exclusive.

Although the polemic has gotten off to a bad start, and it is confused, unjust, and partisan and has produced more heat than light, it has raised fundamental problems that cannot be evaded and that this book endeavors to analyze. Everything revolves around one point: Is the problem Islam in particular or religion in general? In other words, did Christianity help to establish the current secular and political order, even though the church itself has been marginalized, whereas Islam is intrinsically resistant to any form of *laïcité* or even any other variety of secularization? Or are we going through with Islam now what we went through with Catholicism a century ago: a mere question of arrangements, legal constraints, and negotiations, so that a modern, liberal, and European Islam might finally emerge, an Islam that has been domesticated in every sense of the word? Or, rather, has the configuration that gave rise to the assumptions embodied in *laïcité* (a sovereign state that embodies the political sphere confronting a church that proclaims its universality) entered into crisis, making the current attempt to restore a now mythical *laïcité* an exercise in futility?

This book does not deal with religious dogma. It is not concerned with providing *the* proper explication of revealed scripture in any religion. I take for granted the fact that one may not criticize Islam for what is common to every revealed monotheistic religion: there is a truth above humanity; there is a community of believers, known variously as chosen people, *umma*, church, or communion of saints; and there are religious norms the violation of which entails punishment in the other world. But the believer's convictions tell us nothing of the place of religion in society. This book employs two concepts that are not synonymous: secularization and *laïcité*. Secularization is a social phenomenon that requires no political implementation: it comes about when religion ceases to be at the center of human life, even though people still consider themselves believers; the everyday practices of people, like the meaning they give to the world, are no longer constructed under the aegis of transcendence and religion. The final stage of secularization is the disappearance of religion, smoothly and gently accomplished (Europe, for example, experienced a decline in religious observance throughout the nineteenth century). But secularization is not antireligious or anticlerical: people merely stop worshiping and stop talking about religion; it is a process. *Laïcité*, on the contrary, is explicit: it is a political choice that defines the place of religion in an authoritarian, legal manner. *Laïcité* is decreed by the state, which then organizes public space (but it does not necessarily cast religion into the private sphere, contrary to a persistent legend; it rather defines, and thus limits in every sense of the word, the visibility of religion in the public space).

The problem of *laïcité* is that of the separation between the religious sphere and the political sphere at the level of society. A believer obviously does not need to separate the two: his conscience indicates to him the place of each order. Religion does not determine what comes under its own aegis, but the law does with respect to *laïcité*, as society does with respect to secularization. The problem is to determine how religion redefines itself in the face of this change in social and political space, how it adapts to it, opposes it, or creates its own space.

The responses are, of course, complex. Indeed, it is possible to consider the problem in two ways.

You may adopt the classic techniques of apologetics: dissect the arguments of adversaries by pointing out their internal contradictions and their hidden preconceptions. You then take a series of examples from history, dogma, or contemporary writers to demonstrate that, of course, Islam is compatible with modernity and *laïcité*. But this looking-glass polemic, on whichever side of it you are located, has the paradoxical disadvantage of agreeing on a shared assumption, which is thus strengthened by the debate—that there is, in fact, a truth as to what Islam does or does not say and that it is that truth that defines the Muslim. The actor is replaced by a text.

Alternatively, you can go outside the confines of the debate by raising a fundamental question: How does a religion function within the social and political realm? How can a religion determine the conduct of its believers, particularly if it lacks a clergy to establish and disseminate the standards? How do believers reconstruct their religion, with or without the help of theologians?

However, and this has been a commonplace in the sociology of religion since Max Weber, there is no causal relation between dogma and conduct. The prohibition against coveting one's neighbor's wife never put an end to adultery in the Christian world, even though it certainly affected sexual morality. The link between Protestantism and the capitalist ethic asserted by Max Weber did not keep very good Catholics from being excellent heads of companies.[11] Hence what needs to be studied are the operators and mechanisms that enable religion to have an impact on social and political life. Two forms are sometimes confused. On the one hand, there is culture—that is, in the anthropological sense—the entirety of the ways of thinking and acting characteristic of a society. Religion exists only through a culture, which may be perceived as ethnic (Arab culture). In this case, religion has to do with ethnicity, customs, traditions. But how does this culture manifest itself in the conduct of an individual, particularly in a context involving the loss of cultural identity, like that confronted by immigrants? It does not explain the specific conduct of social actors, unless it is understood as some kind of ethnic constant. On the other hand, there is fundamentalism—that is, when religion separates itself from the surrounding cultures and defines itself as pure religion in a system of explicit codes (in its political form, this is called Islamic ideology; in its strictly religious form, it is Salafism). It is this form that appears to be a challenge to *laïcité*, whereas it was unwillingly constructed on the basis of that *laïcité*. It is this dimension that will be the focus of my analysis, because it raises the most significant problem, at the risk of an obvious distortion: fundamentalism touches only a minority of believers, and many people defined sociologically as Muslims have no religious practices. But I have deliberately concentrated on what has caused problems.

We therefore have to make a distinction between what has to do with immigration (that is, the importation of foreign cultures, destined to change or disappear in the course of generations) and what has to do with fundamentalism (an attempt to define a pure religion with no link to any particular culture, hence adaptable to the West, even if that may alter the meaning given to the concept of the West) to understand how we can rethink the connections among Islam, democracy, and *laïcité*. But fundamentalism is systematically associated with the importation of a culture, whereas it is one of the consequences of the crisis of cultures.

The question is therefore not so much to find out what it is possible to learn about the past (the history of the Muslim world) as to understand how Islam has today been reconstructed by Muslims. But this reconstruction is seldom carried out on the basis of work by thinkers, theologians, or philosophers; it is carried out in the concrete practices of Muslims immersed in Western society, but also with the help of organic intellectuals like Tariq Ramadan, who provide a language, formulations that simultaneously make it possible to live concretely and to maintain the identity of a true believer in a secularized world. Such language is ambiguous by definition and not out of malice: dual language is, in fact, a recognition of two spaces, that of religion and that of the order of the world, even if this is done with a longing for unity.

There is no abstract process of secularization: what you are after you have left religion is clearly marked by the particular religion you have left, and the forms and spaces of secularization are defined by reference to each particular religion. These spaces are the product of a history and also of a religious history. Religion inhabits society: religion has shaped society, and it returns either in a secularized form or, on the contrary, in outbreaks of fundamentalism.

It is difficult to understand the strength and success of Communist movements in western Europe without seeing in them the ghosts of a thoroughly Christian eschatology and church. Our *laïcité* and our secularization are both in their way Christian, because they were built on the basis of Christianity: How many major philosophers of the Middle Ages were members of the clergy, including those who, like William of Ockham, argued for the subordination of religious power to temporal authority? How many apostles of *laïcité*, like Émile Combes, had a thoroughly religious education? But it would be very ethnocentric to make French *laïcité* the model for the exit from religion: it was first of all the assertion of a strong state, which itself was considered sacred. It makes no sense in English-speaking common law countries, where the state, not at all weak, is not invested with the mission to construct society and embody its thinking. And yet those countries experienced secularization without *laïcité*. This is even more true for Muslim societies, which have produced their own forms of secularization: nothing in the way in which politics functions is Islamic in itself, but law and customs have been profoundly affected by Islam. The question in the Muslim world has therefore never been the place of the church but that of sharia, but the imposition of sharia tends precisely to divest the state of a part of what is seen in the West as its prerogative: the monopoly of legislation (although in the United States the growing role of the judiciary in the definition of social bonds and the quasi-privatization of the law by the legal profession also point in the same direction). It is therefore clear that it is futile to think of *laïcité* as a simple relation between state and religion; it sets out the way in which society defines itself politically. Our secularized societies are haunted by religion. There are therefore separate histories of the establishment of *laïcité* and of secularization, and it would do no good to establish a definitive model. Being greeted at Heathrow by a British customs agent wearing a veil shows the French traveler that it is obviously not the same Islam that poses a problem for British democracy.

The problem arises when globalization introduces a gap among concrete societies, cultural models, and political structures, that is, when a model is detached from the historic conditions in which it was produced: this is the case for the modern state, for the rights of man, and for democracy, which are exportable, but probably not for *laïcité*, which is deeply rooted in the history of modern France. The question then arises of the compatibility of those forms, now considered universal, with religions and cultures perceived as particularist, especially in the context of Muslim immigration. But what is less noticed is that religion has also become detached from the historical, social, and cultural conditions that brought it into being and rooted it in relatively stable cultures. We therefore continue to think about *laïcité* and religion as the expression of political cultures, not seeing that their universalization depends precisely on their loss of cultural identity. But religion and *laïcité* are both invoked today in the name of identity and set forth as opposing mirror images of each other. And yet they are being rebuilt by ignoring their historical roots, which paradoxically makes them less incompatible than one might think, because they are fluctuating, are productive of diverse spaces, and embody principles that sit side by side rather than in opposition to each other.

The religious phenomenon is no longer the bearer of a political alternative; the conflict is not a conflict of legitimacy between religion and the state but the symptom of the appearance of new spaces that cannot be confined within a territory, a society, a nation, and a state. Religion today is participating, in the same way as the construction of Europe is, in the disassembly of the spaces that created the modern nation-state. This may be cause for regret or rejoicing, or we may simply draw the necessary conclusions to think in a different way about the place of religion. But demonization of the other is only a different, and more sinister, way of practicing religion.

I

FRENCH *LAÏCITÉ* AND ISLAM
Which Is the Exception?

Secularization Is Not the Same Thing as *Laïcité*

How is it possible to define the relationship between two terms as vague and controversial as *laïcité* and "Islam"? We know that *laïcité* is a characteristically French phenomenon, incomprehensible in Great Britain, where customs agents and police officers are permitted to wear veils, as well as in the United States, where no president can be elected who does not speak of God. And yet both those countries are Western secular democracies. The question of *laïcité* thus raises two distinct problems: one is the identity and particularity of France and the other the relationship between Islam, on one side, and "secularization" and democracy, on the other. At the outset, we must draw a distinction between secularization, whereby a society emancipates itself from a sense of the sacred that it does not necessarily deny, and *laïcité*, whereby the state expels religious life beyond a border that the state itself has defined by law.[1] In fact, situations differ considerably, depending on variations in two parameters: the separation of church and state (yes or no) and the position of religion in society (strong or weak). A country may be secular but not *laïque*, because it has an official religion (Great Britain, Denmark); it may even be *laïque* (strictly asserting the separation of church and state) while simultaneously recognizing the role of religion in the public sphere (the United States, where the Supreme Court recently upheld the recitation of "under God" in the Pledge of Allegiance in public schools); in a state described as *laïque* like Turkey, where the law contains no reference to Islam, there is, in fact, no separation of church and state, because imams are government employees, as are pastors in Denmark.

Likewise, when we speak of Islam, what are we referring to? The dogma? But that is a matter of debate and a variety of interpretations among Muslims themselves: they all assert that there is only one Islam, but each has his own personal analysis, ranging from a liberalism that rejects the veil and would not turn down a drink to a fundamentalism that kills the spirit in the name of the letter. It is thus always possible to identify polemically the "true" Islam of one's choosing: fundamentalist, liberal, even secular.[2] Are we referring to the culture and history of the Arab Muslim world? But as a matter of fact, Islam has now left the Middle East, and that is why the question of its relationship to French *laïcité* has arisen. We can, of course, consider democratization in the Middle East and the relationship between democracy and Islam, but we ought not to forget that the principal obstacles to democracy in the Middle East are posed by secular regimes (Tunisia, Baathist Syria, the Front de libération nationale [National Liberation Front] and the army in Algeria, Egypt) and that their political model (one party and president for life) is borrowed from European fascism or Third World socialism, very distant from the Koran and the tradition of the Prophet. Moreover, does speaking of Islam as a unitary phenomenon really enable us to understand the concrete practices of people known as Muslims? In what way is the element "Islam" relevant to an understanding of the underlying motive forces of modern societies, even Muslim societies? All this leads to little but the rehashing of a few tired clichés.

Of course, when we speak of the relationship between Islam and *laïcité* in the Western world, we always have in mind the symmetry with (or opposition to) Christianity. For the West, secularization and *laïcité* alike were established alongside, or rather against, Christianity. Is the same story being repeated with Islam as in 1905, when veiled women were driven from public places by force of arms (then it was Catholic nuns), or is there something specific about Islam that makes it incompatible with our *laïcité*? A parallel is often drawn between the way the French Republic manages Christianity or Judaism and its current confrontation with Islam, but usually to show the irreducible difference that Islam embodies. But if there is a structural incompatibility between Islam and *laïcité*, we would need to explain in what way that is not true for other religions. We would, for example, like Islam to experience a religious reformation like Protestantism, while we forget that Catholicism has laboriously adapted to modernity and neglected any such reformation. It is argued that Christianity has always accepted a secular space ("Render unto Caesar . . ."), while forgetting that the churches (from Gregory the Great to Calvin) claimed the right to define and control that space. The establishment of such a space is first of all a political act: French *laïcité* was indeed built against the Catholic Church, but not necessarily against religion, although for the most dedicated rationalists the two went hand in hand, and for many secular people today the expression of religious feeling remains a threat and a scandal, as we saw in the rejection of Rocco Buttiglione as European commissioner because he openly expressed very conservative religious positions.

Instead of getting lost in cultural and theological debates that might shed light on the past but are irrelevant to what is meaningful today, we ought to reconsider the constant oscillation between secularization, whereby society gradually emancipates itself from religion without necessarily denying it, and *laïcité*, in which the political authority closes off the space of religion the better to define public space as its opposite. We have to say clearly what is the problem for our *laïcité*: Some particular religion or all religion? And to do that, we have to reconsider the very matrix of the relationship between the republic and religion in general.

French *Laïcité*: A Legal and Political Principle

Why is *laïcité* such a burning subject in France? The first reason is probably that the debate touches on what is considered the heart of French identity, at a moment when that identity has been challenged from above by European integration. Consequently, we cling to a pseudoconsensus on republican and national values, which seem to be dissolving from below, in the *banlieues* and the schools. At bottom, Islam is not the cause of the crisis of the French model but the mirror in which society now sees itself. France is experiencing the crisis of its identity through Islam. The second reason is that different meanings are attached to the concept of *laïcité*. But the problem here is not so much to define the true meaning of *laïcité* as to determine how it creates meaning in our society. The supporters of *laïcité* are far from sharing a single view; there is a large distance between advocates of an open and modest *laïcité*, like Jean Baubérot, and defenders of *laïcité* defined as a comprehensive project (Henri Peña-Ruiz).[3] I see three registers in which the word is used.

Laïcité *as a Philosophy*

This goes far beyond the separation of church and state and implies a conception of values, of society, of the nation, and of the republic, based on the philosophy of the Enlightenment, the idea of progress, and finally advocacy of an ethics not rooted in religion but proclaimed as rationalist. This philosophy has, of course, imbued the teaching profession and school textbooks since Jules Ferry and has become the consensus view of the Left.[4] A good contemporary expression of the view can be found in the works of Henri Peña-Ruiz and the writings of Didier Motchane (who was an adviser to Jean-Pierre Chevènement when he was interior minister).[5] It will not be discussed here, because it is in fact an opinion, a perfectly respectable one, but one that it would be groundless to set up as a standard or an official truth. Ideologies are like religions: there are those that appear more amiable, more open, more tolerant or that are more familiar to us because they are rooted in our upbringing, but they are conceptually closed systems, because they define themselves as hegemonic (since religion is acceptable in this instance only if it is integrated into this system of values); the limit of the hegemony is tolerance, but tolerance presupposes hierarchy—you tolerate by including, by making the other's thinking a subset of the whole. By definition, there can be no consensus on *laïcité* as a philosophy, because many believers—whatever their religion—cannot recognize themselves in it. If we want to leave the religious realm, we must not make *laïcité* into a religion. I see no reason to combat one ideological discourse with another, when my intention is to determine under what conditions it is possible to refrain from ideological discourse.

Many advocates of political *laïcité* have developed philosophical thinking on the subject, but a study of the secular coalition that finally imposed the separation of church and state in 1905 shows that it was never driven by a consensus on a philosophical or an ideological conception of *laïcité* and that its members had very varied allegiances and motivations.[6] Secular thinking is an afterthought that does, of course, have a philosophical history, but it is not the origin of the politics of *laïcité*.[7] *Laïcité* is a body of laws before being a system of thought.

Laïcité *as an Effect of the Law*

The notion of *laïcité* as a legal principle is open to question, because it is never defined as such by the text of a law.[8] The 1905 law establishing separation did not use the word *laïcité*. It was not until the Constitution of 1946 that the word appeared explicitly as a constitutional principle entailing legal effects, but without being further specified. The reality of *laïcité* is, however, clearly legal, because, after all the debates, parliament by passing laws and the courts by applying the laws and through jurisprudence define what is required of citizens: *laïcité* is known through the law. We may therefore conclude that *laïcité* is defined by the body of statutes making up the French law of religion, interpreted by jurisprudence. *Laïcité* is what may be inferred as the common principle of all the laws that have regulated the place of religion in the French public square since the assertion of the principle of the separation of church and state. In the eyes of the law, *laïcité* is neither a state of mind nor a philosophy nor even a principle, but a body of laws that derive their validity—of course—from the will of the legislature: its truth is thus political.[9]

Laïcité *as a Political Principle*

Laïcité in France is tied to a precise historical and political context: the determination to disengage the state and society from the influence of the Catholic Church, more than from religion in general. The republic was finally constructed in opposition to the Catholic Church. French *laïcité* is historically a matter of dispute between the republican state and the Catholic Church, founded on anticlericalism. It is thus a combative *laïcité* marked by verbal violence and anathema, which has recurred today in the polemics on Islam. Broadly speaking, this conflict lasted from 1790, the year of the imposition of the Civil Constitution of the Clergy, to 1924, the year when the church accepted the 1905 law. It has persisted in the sphere of education. The atmosphere of ideological civil war that France experienced from 1790 to 1981 (or, rather, 1984, with the huge demonstration in favor of private schools) hinged almost entirely on the question of the political position of the Catholic Church; in fact, the defense of *laïcité* has probably been the only common denominator of all the parties of the Left. In parallel with this political establishment of *laïcité*, the church's acceptance of the republic and of *laïcité* was political, not theological. The recognition of the republic by the Catholic Church (the "toast of Algiers" delivered at the pope's instigation by Cardinal Lavigerie in November 1890) had nothing to do with new theological speculation; it was a purely political decision, motivated by political considerations. The Vatican's belated acceptance of the 1905 law (in 1924), once the republic had agreed to recognize the hierarchical structure of the Catholic Church—that is, the bishop's control over parishes through the diocesan organization—was also a political decision. It was through the dissociation between the political and the theological that the separation became acceptable, but this dissociation was not a matter of course: the popes at first condemned it, but the fear that Catholics would be marginalized or that they would undertake the construction of a Catholic party, dragging the church into partisan disputes, persuaded the papacy and the majority of the clergy to accept the new political order precisely so that it would be neutral and not an instrument for the imposition of a vision of the world. The question of *laïcité* is primarily political.

The subsequent emergence of Christian Democracy signaled the real—not opportunistic—adhesion of Catholics to the republic. The church attempted to rediscover common ground for the definition of moral values with nonpracticing citizens, clinging sometimes to the notion of natural law, sometimes to that of the Christian culture of Europe (as Pope John Paul II did in 2004 when he asked that a reference to Christian culture be incorporated into the preamble of the European Constitution), and even, for the Catholic Left, by developing what is known as liberation theology. But the peace treaty was not immediately concluded: twentieth-century France, in its unions, civic associations, and schools—that is, in civil society—was deeply divided between *laïcs* and *cathos* (and only Catholics, because Jews and Protestants were on the side of the *laïcs*). Behind the false unanimity of the public school, there were two kinds of networks for sociability, union organization, and even leisure activities (sports clubs, holiday celebrations, summer camps, scouting, youth groups, informal universities, lecture series, and so on): the secular and the church-sponsored, with greater or lesser antagonism depending on the region. Of course, there were sometimes mixed marriages, as there are today, but people lived in two different worlds. The French Communist Party had, in its way, sectarianized the *banlieues* (and hardly shared certain republican values, such as parliamentary democracy). Even though the political choices made by each group grew less distinct (with the Resistance and the development of a Catholicism of the Left), the split affected ways of thinking (we know how little the "second Left," often led by men from Christian backgrounds, was ever able to make itself acceptable to the Socialist Party). This conflict focused on the question of education, which faded only between 1984 (the year when the Left accepted private schools) and 1994 (the year when the Right stopped seeking the revenge of the private school). One might wonder, moreover, whether the end of the conflict over education is connected with the rise, if not of Islam, at least of violence in the *banlieues*, with leftist members of the middle classes finding in private schools a means of getting around the rigidities of the residential assignment of schools, which they had always supported. In any event, at the very moment when a split that was two centuries old was fading, a new one appeared: *laïcité* against Islam (or vice versa). It was as though the old pattern of conflict were inherent in French identity and only the religious agent had changed.

Laïcité thus refers back first of all to the structuring of French political space, which was carried out in conflict and polemics but helped to forge and stabilize French identities, which went well beyond the ballot (from the Communist to the Catholic, including the Radical Socialist along the way). French *laïcité* is inseparable from the construction of the republican state from the Revolution on. It also no doubt served to create a "class alliance" to sidestep the troublesome social question.[10] It certainly still plays the same role of blurring social divisions to the extent that the criticism of Islam cuts across class lines and touches very varied political, social, and religious circles but also to the extent that it adopts a primarily cultural perspective on the complex realities of the *banlieues*. This very close bond between republic and *laïcité* is a product of French history, but it has been so far internalized that we have invented the myth of a consensus on republican values. Political choice has logically been expressed by a body of laws, but it has also been surrounded by a philosophical (others would say ideological) elaboration of *laïcité*, which there is even less reason to make into a normative system because it is, in fact, very complex (many *laïcs*, especially in the nineteenth century, thought of themselves as the defenders of a certain religious idea against Catholic clericalism).

Oddly enough, then, today's *laïcité* is based on the myth of consensus, particularly the consensus on republican values. This is doubly a myth because one wonders, first of all, about what there was a consensus about (between a Stalinist of the 1950s and a Catholic opposed to Vatican II, for example) and, second, since it is obvious that there are citizens who do not seem to join in the consensus, whether the latter should be considered excluded from the political order (or excluding themselves, which amounts to the same thing). Civil war is not far off because, while the republic is founded on a consensus, which remains to be demonstrated, whoever does not adopt it is not inside the republic.

But Jules Ferry's consensus was negative: the elementary-school teacher was to say nothing that might shock a father (*laïcité* was also patriarchal; today we would add the mother).[11] *Laïcité* aimed not to exclude believers but to define a space of neutrality. If there is a consensus, it is not on values but on respect for a rule of the game, insofar as it is ratified by the popular will. The consensus concerns the political and constitutional principle of *laïcité*, not philosophy. We see, among other things, how the Catholic Church defends fundamental values against legislative choices, for example, in opposing abortion. And if that opposition does not lead to civil war, this is because the two parties accept precisely that the debate will not turn into opposition to the political system. The law does not ask that the archbishop of Paris approve of abortion: a priest in the pulpit may condemn it and say that it is a sin and a crime. But any encouragement of or support for an attack on clinics conducting abortions is a criminal offense. There is a very clear line between actions and opinions, and it must stay that way. But it is, in fact, becoming blurred because of the recent tendency to criminalize opinions (the Gayssot law on racism, anti-Semitism, and xenophobia; the law on homophobia), which means that even if one starts from a republican consensus (revisionism is unacceptable), one arrives very soon at a policing of ideas.

Laïcité thus ought to be negative above all: it aims at freeing political, but also public, space from religious control. But it does not aim to replace religious discourse by a new ethics: such an idea is totally absent from the body of laws that defines *laïcité*. And this touches on a very important aspect of French *laïcité*: because it is based on the separation of church and state, it is absolutely forbidden for it to speak of dogma. This is at least the theory.

It might be thought that there are hence no grounds for raising the question of the theological compatibility of any particular religion with *laïcité*. And yet the debate now concerns theology more than ever.

Laïcité's Unspoken Thought: The Fascination of Theology

The recurrent question in this book is to determine why we question Islam about dogma, whereas we hold that Christian dogma is compatible with *laïcité* or that the church's political acceptance of *laïcité* exonerates it from any suspicion about theological content. Dual language or observation of a fact: Muslim dogma is thought to pose a problem that Christianity does not. Essayists and politicians summon Islam to give pledges: they want an Islam *à la française*, liberal, even . . . secular.[12] Some therefore assert that we have to foster this Islam, while others suggest that at bottom Islam is by definition not compatible with *laïcité*. More deeply, there arises the question of all forms of fundamentalism: Can some be absorbed into the republic, or do we have to struggle against all fundamentalism (defined here as the requirement that the believer fully live his faith, that is, submit all activities of his life, including social and political activities, to a religious standard)? While these questions may be legitimate on the intellectual level, they pose a political problem: Should the state take dogma into consideration?

French *laïcité* forbids it. The state has no call to intervene in dogma: the courts and the Conseil d'État frequently reiterate this point, emphasizing that when the state must intervene—for example, on vaccinations and transfusions for Jehovah's Witnesses—it take into account only public order or the interests of the child (because he is a minor) but never question dogma. And this is true even when the dogma asserts things that are in contradiction with the law. This is, moreover, a constant of jurisprudence: a woman may not sue the Catholic Church for sexual discrimination because she has been prevented from studying in a seminary and being ordained as a priest. In addition, ordinary law does not apply to the internal organization of churches (a priest deprived of his priesthood by the bishop cannot sue for wrongful dismissal). For the same reason, there is no ground for the state to challenge religious dogmas in Islam (apostasy, prohibition of marriage between a Muslim woman and a non-Muslim man, and so on), except to prosecute someone relying on a principle of the kind to commit the actual offense of inciting a crime or committing a crime himself.[13]

It would therefore suffice to hold to this principle so as not to pose the question of dogma, all the more because, as the *Traité du droit français des religions* demonstrates, Islam raises no specific problems that would require new legislation: current laws and jurisprudence suffice to deal with the particular cases posed by Islam (besides, very few Muslim community leaders have asked for a modification of the 1905 law, which has rather been suggested by Christians—including Pastor de Clermont—and by Nicolas Sarkozy).[14]

Yet the entire debate today concerns dogma from several angles. First, the question of the selection of members of the Conseil français du culte musulman (French Council of the Muslim Faith): Should the largest organizations be favored, although they are close to Salafist circles, such as the Union des organisations islamiques de France (UOIF; Union of Islamic Organizations of France) (recognizing the differences, this reminds us that the state has always had a weakness for strong, centralized, and organized unions, which by definition are very dogmatic, like the Confédération générale du travail [General Confederation of Labor]), or rather "liberal" figures? The political choice here presupposes a choice between religious interpretations. There then arises the question of the training of ministers of the religion: the call, which has now become ritual, for the training of French imams is meaningful only if one assumes that those imams will be more liberal than imported fundamentalists or the self-proclaimed young imams of the *banlieues*. The demand for the reform of the dogmas, in this case formulated outside state bodies, also comes from intellectuals engaged in the debate on Islam. For example, Michèle Tribalat and Jeanne-Hélène Kaltenbach, in their book *La République et l'Islam*, are indignant that the Ministry of the Interior withdrew from a proposal to consult Muslim authorities about the reference to an oath of allegiance to republican laws and especially the explicit mention of the right to change religions.[15] But here, too, such a step would be completely contrary to legal *laïcité*: an oath makes sense only in a regime governed by concordat; asking for the renunciation of what some consider to be a part of dogma (the condemnation of apostasy) is not within the state's province.

The paradox is that Tariq Ramadan's celebrated declaration calling for a moratorium on the application of *hudud* (corporal punishments explicitly provided by sharia for certain "crimes against

God") is much more in conformity with the concept of *laïcité* than the requirement that the very principle of these divine commandments be renounced.[16] The state has no knowledge of the heavenly kingdom and legislates only on terrestrial matters; it is therefore important for it that no sentence of corporal punishment be pronounced and even less executed here below. Hell can wait. The moratorium is a good compromise, to be sure a bit hypocritical, but what religion is not when it has to deal with earthly political realities? And yet this declaration was greeted with jubilation by those opposed to Ramadan, because they saw it as proof that he was using a dual language. In fact, however, he asserted (1) that one cannot change the law of God, and (2) that the law of the state is the one that prevails in the world. What bishop would say the contrary? Of course, out of concern not to stigmatize Islam alone, one might accompany the criticism of Islam with an attack against Christianity or Judaism (as some extreme secularists such as Jocelyn Bézecourt in fact do). One might, for example, always consider that Christian theology is inegalitarian and discriminatory and demand not only the right of women to be priests but also the abolition of hell, because it discriminates against nonbelievers (but the invention of purgatory by the Catholic Church is a step in that direction, because it is nothing but, as Ramadan would say, a long moratorium). Similarly, it would be a good idea to demand that the Calvinists give up the concept of predestination (which asserts that God has chosen those who will be saved or damned from the moment of their birth), because the damned, condemned even before coming into existence, have access to no appeal procedure. And we could ask the Jews to give up the idea of the "chosen people" (interestingly enough, by the way, the notion is often invoked, precisely by those who slide from anti-Zionism into anti-Semitism, for the purpose of defining Israel as a racist state: the manipulation of theology for purposes of political demonization does not affect Islam alone).

The debate, in fact, clearly illustrates an ambiguity in French *laïcité* that goes back to 1790 and the Civil Constitution of the

Clergy but resurfaced with the policy consistently followed by all interior ministers since Pierre Joxe set up the Conseil représentatif de l'Islam de France (CORIF; Representative Council of Islam in France) in 1989—that the state get involved precisely in the organization of religion and by doing so try to influence religious choices by the selection of its interlocutors. Instead of taking offense at this confusion, the supporters of strict *laïcité* criticize it for not going far enough by not excluding "fundamentalists." The slogan of Islam *à la française*, or French Islam, is explicitly aimed at favoring a liberal or even secular Islam—that is, of emptying any religion not necessarily of its transcendence but of its demand for the absolute.

The unspoken thought of *laïcité à la française* is, in fact, the control of the religious by the political sphere, following either a Caesaropapist model—where the sovereign intervenes in theological matters—or a Gallican one—where the Church of France, encouraged by the state, jurisdictionally frees itself from Rome. It was not an accident that to set up the CORIF, Pierre Joxe chose Alain Boyer, a high-ranking government official and *agrégé* in history, who had studied the establishment of the grand Sanhedrin by the emperor Napoleon, who wanted to create an institution to represent and control the Jews of France. This model of the authoritarian organization of the Jewish community within the framework of the French state is, in fact, frequently cited to explain how one may proceed to integrate a religion without churches and with a strong communitarian tradition. The problem is that the establishment of what was to become the Consistoire israélite (umbrella organization of French Jews) was carried out in the framework of an authoritarian empire operating under a concordat—that is, the complete opposite of a secular democratic republic. The republic is never very far from the authoritarian temptation: in the concordat period (before 1905), the republican state punished priests who refused to give communion for reasons that were deemed to be political.[17] The recent deportation of imams for mere statements seems to point in the same direction. The impulse to control also affects the educational system. The organization of a course of study of Islam by the state, frequently mentioned by the authorities but always put off, was, to be sure, never openly aimed at propagating an Islam *à la française*, but officials did hint at the possibility: "But the responsibility incumbent on [the state] does not amount to organizing training in Islam, in other words, the education of imams, but in fact to developing knowledge of Islam in our country (it being clearly understood that one may anticipate that the development of such knowledge is one of the conditions that will give Muslims in France the possibility of recruiting their imams in their own country)."[18]

The oath of allegiance for ministers of religion, briefly contemplated by the High Council for Integration in 2000 for Muslims alone, was imposed by the Civil Constitution of the Clergy of 1790 on all priests (when the country was officially subject to a concordat). It was rejected by the papacy, which divided the clergy between those who swore the oath and the refractory, who were severely repressed. This kind of oath is presecular: it fits into the Gallican determination to control religious institutions. Applying it to Muslims alone would, in addition, be discriminatory (and would have automatically been nullified by the Conseil d'État). Similarly, the 1905 law provides that the state not intervene in the internal organization of religious institutions, but this is precisely what the Interior Ministry has done by setting up the Conseil français du culte musulman. This is not a criticism of the substance of the policy pursued but simply a way of pointing out that if you want to adopt a *laïcité* with rules that vary for political reasons, this predominance of the political ought to be openly accepted, not hidden behind some purported philosophical essence of *laïcité* and a sacrosanct respect for the 1905 law, the spirit, if not the letter, of which is violated by this approach.

Moreover, if we consider the history of the 1905 law, we clearly see that some secular politicians hesitated at the idea of separating church and state precisely because it would deprive the state of a means of control.[19] This was the point of view of Mustafa Kemal Atatürk in Turkey: his secularism was very militant and would have been openly antireligious had the influence of Islam in his country not compelled him to be more cautious. He therefore chose not the separation of church and state but the control of religion by the state (the imams are under an office of religious affairs, the Dyanet, that pays their salaries and even composes sermons). One can sense a longing for this kind of state-directed *laïcité* in many contemporary French commentators.

But can we speak of an antireligious *laïcité*? It is clear that for many secular activists the problem is indeed religion: for example, when they sincerely argue that religion is a purely private affair, which is not at all the definition provided in the law.[20] The 1905 law provides for the conduct of worship in public space (and it, of course, organizes it): religious edifices are public, processions are conducted in public, chaplains also carry out their activities in public places (schools, prisons, barracks), protocol assigns a place to representatives of religions, and priestly dress is not prohibited in public places (it was discovered at the start of classes in the fall of 2004 in some lycées in Var that chaplains had been showing up for years in cassocks: the administration banned them only then out of concern for the parallel with the prohibition of the veil, but it had not previously been a problem—yet another sign that Islam is in fact the problem). Some heads of schools have been so zealous as to bar entry to mothers wearing veils, whereas others are not content with refusing to have *hallal* meat in their cafeterias (which remains within the framework of *laïcité*) but want Muslim children to eat non-*hallal* meat (which goes far beyond it).[21]

The Gallican Temptation as a Palliative for Communitarization

There is clearly a continuity in the affirmation of *laïcité* in France: most teachers who refuse to have veiled students in class would be just as intransigent against seminarians in cassocks (well, almost: it took the law on the veil to bring to their notice that there were

Sikh students wearing turbans and chaplains wearing cassocks). The phobia against sects has sometimes served to justify a full-scale attack against innocent followers of more or less harmless practices. But in the end, *laïcité* had managed to find a compromise with established religions. The abrupt appearance of new forms of religiosity starting in the 1970s changed everything. The 1980s were a turning point; just when militant *laïcité* seemed about to disappear for want of opponents, it reconstructed itself around a new enemy, Islam. At a time when the conflict with the Catholic Church was dying down, new forms of religious affirmation appeared, not all of which, incidentally, were connected to Islam: Sephardic Jews repatriated from Algeria injected more demonstrative piety into French Judaism, evangelical Protestantism and the charismatic movement placed the question of faith in the forefront and left the four walls of churches to show themselves in the streets, sects flourished, and, finally, Islam became a massive presence.

But reactions to these revivalist movements varied. The community of Taizé was popular, but the sects were disturbing. It was interesting to see hostility develop in particular cases, such as sects suspected of infiltration and the formation of parallel networks in power centers (Scientology, for example; the Freemasons, too, were not exempt from this suspicion, judging by the number of features that weeklies published about them). But another form of rejection appeared when there was an ostensible occupation of public space by a specific group (especially when it was overdetermined by an ethnic element), even if the law was respected: for example, evangelical assemblies of Gypsies, when tens of thousands of people converged on airfields leased for the occasion, caused local mayors to mobilize (whereas the annual procession of Gypsies in Saintes-Maries-de-la-Mer was integrated into tradition and indeed folklore); also worth mentioning is the construction of regional worship and meeting centers (the Jehovah's Witnesses in Montreuil in Eure-et-Loir, for example), as well, of course, as the construction of mosques. The title of a book, *Les Territoires perdus de la république,* says a good deal about this basically territorial view of society as being whittled away at by the "other."[22] The prohibition of the veil in school and the question of *hallal* meat in school cafeterias should be seen more in light of this notion of territorial reconquest than as a defense of neutrality.

It is therefore natural for Islam to lie at the heart of this anxiety, because it has a demographic weight beyond that of other movements. But it causes anxiety in two different registers: the communitarian ghetto and triumphant proselytism. The *banlieue* and the world, the local and the global: Islam is present at both extremities where national identity seems to be crumbling. Islam's proselytism causes anxiety, as if by definition a universalistic religion did not have a vocation to convert. Islam is perceived as a potential factor of profound change in society. The idea is that, given the demographic weight of Muslims, any process of communitarization would bring about a profound imbalance in French society: first by fragmenting society from below but also by plugging the "ghettos" into a universal Islam that is not bound by the framework of the nation-state. We are thus caught between two visions: an ethnic Islam (Arab, Middle Eastern) that would import the conflicts of the Middle East into France, and a nonethnic and supranational Islam, specifically European. The foil in this second instance is less the Middle East than the very dissolution of the national framework of the state in favor of supranational institutions and identities. The question of Islam is thus intimately related to that of sovereignty, of Europe and the debate about the nation-state, globalization, the deterritorialization of conflicts, and the crisis of identity. At bottom, the growth of Islam is intuitively seen as part of the process of globalization and deterritorialization (and contemporary Salafism is surfing that wave). The response is thus a demand for the nationalization of Islam, or else its secularization. The ambiguity here (and what differentiates it from the right-wing anti-Semitism of the 1930s) is that many on the Left consider it urgent (hence possible) to de-Islamize immigration: integration, indeed assimilation, remains the objective, but Islam is seen as an obstacle. We have nothing against immigrants (at least for now), but we want secular Muslims. The intervention of the republican state into religious affairs thus seems justified by this combat situation. Many books published recently in France contain explicit calls to sanction fellow travelers, the naive, the lukewarm, the soft, the fascinated, and so on. In a word, in light of the failure of the intelligentsia, it is up to the state to take things in hand. There is talk of resistance to "Islamo-fascism." There are recurrent comparisons to Munich in 1938, but many who take themselves for Churchill write like Céline, without his style.

The defense of *laïcité* is more than ever the defense of an identity that has difficulty defining itself positively because, as we have seen, it is largely based on myths, including the myth of consensus. In particular, the debate on *laïcité*, now as in 1905, makes it possible to obscure the social question: if the *banlieue* is primarily a problem of Islam, then there is no social problem. This is, in fact, an old tradition of French social democracy: to use *laïcité* to evade a debate on the economy. The problems of society are transformed into a debate about ideas. And consequently, ideas become the quarry of a witch hunt (as shown in the campaigns against Tariq Ramadan and Xavier Ternisien). The circulation of ideas is thus attributed to the activity of certain individuals, and the old clichés of the cold war return (like that of contagion, transforming ideas into viruses). There is no analysis of why some ideas work, whereas the market of religion contains not only a supply but also a demand. It is interesting to note that this is practically the same reasoning that is applied to sects: the most prominent explanation is the influence of a guru and mental manipulation. A young girl wearing a veil is necessarily manipulated, and the paradox is that we repress her the better to liberate her: since the veil is a sign of enslavement, a woman could not possibly choose it voluntarily. The same reasoning drove the French Revolution to prohibit religious orders, because a free person could not voluntarily alienate his own freedom.

And yet God knows (He especially) that voluntary slavery exists. Emancipating people despite themselves is another paradox.

What is often the expression of a personal choice (wearing the veil) is seen as the consequence of social pressure. This optical illusion clearly shows that the obsession is with communitarianization. The determination to intervene in religious matters is aimed at "liberating" the Muslim woman (whether from the veil or from an arranged marriage). The woman question is indeed central in communitarianism: social control of the group over women, beyond the question of custom, involves the question of marriage and hence of the perpetuation of the community. Once again, however, the desire to preserve endogamy is not specific to Islam; it is found in religious Jewish communities, and that creates no political difficulties: the denunciation of mixed marriages is a constant for Conservative rabbis and poses well-known problems in Israeli nationality law (Orthodox rabbis recognize only descent from the mother and reject conversions of convenience). The difference between reactions provoked by the same conduct dictated by similar reasons (to preserve a religious community) clearly shows that it is the nature of those communities that causes the problem and not so much the communitarian phenomenon in itself. The community of practicing Jews is not (or no longer) seen as expanding, and contemporary anti-Semitism is based on myths other than that of demographic expansion ("They are everywhere," a recurrent theme in the 1930s). But the question of Muslim communitarianism cannot be separated from its demographic dimension.

As a consequence, the problems in general posed by the *banlieues*, integration (or its failure), communitarianism, and the like are attributed to the religious element, Islam. Far from cordoning off religion, militant *laïcité* constantly brings it back to the center of the debate and makes it the explanation for social disorders. If *banlieues* turn in on themselves, if adolescents wear particular costumes to express an identity or use a demand for a particular kind of food to express opposition in school, this is the fault of

Islam. Religion is seen as a cause, not a symptom, and as a result the response is made in religious terms, thereby definitively turning it into a mark of identity and of protest.

Laïcité is, above all, an obsession with religion, and it leads to the desire to legislate about religion instead of accepting true separation: hence the tendencies of republicans of every stripe toward Caesaropapism, Gallicanism, or even a restoration of the concordat system (Nicolas Sarkozy, at the time interior minister, went to Cairo to solicit from the mufti of the Egyptian Republic a *nihil obstat* for the prohibition of the veil), the syndrome of a republic not comfortable in its skin, because it is as fascinated by monarchy as it is by religion.

But we are not talking about just any religion. There is in French *laïcité* a specific fear of Islam, whether we seek to de-Islamize immigration or, on the contrary, to reject immigration and the generations of the French descended from it in the name of an alleged incompatibility between Islam and Western values. But the only thing that is specifically French is precisely the use of the system of *laïcité* to domesticate Islam. Other Western countries use other systems, also based on the idea that there is a political rule of the game, but one that is much less intrusive with regard to the belief and the person of the other: multiculturalism, interfaith dialogue, the rights of minorities, and so on. But if the contrast was very sharp in the 1980s between the assimilationist approach *à la française*—legally based on the principle of *laïcité* but, in fact, deeply rooted in a political concept of the nation—and the multiculturalist approach of northern Europe, the turn of the century was marked by a crisis of both models: France was brought to recognize a Muslim religious reality that it would rather ignore (positively with the establishment of the Conseil français du culte musulman in 2002 and negatively with the prohibition of the veil in 2004), while Holland, shattered by the assassination of the filmmaker Theo Van Gogh in November 2004 by a young Muslim of Moroccan origin but Dutch citizenship, confronted the failure of positive multiculturalism (cultures are good and should coexist) and turned toward a negative vision of that same multiculturalism (some cultures, like Islam, are difficult to integrate), without calling into question a view based on the issue of culture (whereas very clearly, as I shall show, the radicalism in question is a product of the loss of cultural identity).

In fact, disquiet in the face of Islam is real in all Western countries but is shaped and experienced according to the patterns derived from the political culture of each of them. The elements that are found shocking are completely different from one country to another, but each attributes to Islam an essence that is heterogeneous to the essence of Western culture. Which introduces a slightly paradoxical element: we reject Islam for very different reasons, but they all create a kind of negative European identity. For example, the veil is a focus of French rejection but causes no problems in Great Britain, which, in contrast, prohibits the ritual slaughter of animals (*hallal*), for the same reasons that it has banned fox hunting, whereas in France the source of the problem is not the form of slaughter (except for Brigitte Bardot) but the lack of organization with which it is carried out. It is probably not an accident that Pym Fortuyn, the Islamophobic Dutch politician, was shot by a defender of animals: the question of the protection of animals in northern Europe seems to activists to be intimately related to the defense of human rights, which seems simply inconceivable in southern Europe. The reaction against Islam is formulated very differently from one European country to the next, which means that, taken one by one, the elements that seem incompatible between Islam and the West (the veil, *hallal*) are not really so, including those having to do with the woman question: when the Italian nominee to the European Commission in October 2004, Rocco Buttiglione, declared that he thought woman's place was in the home under the protection of her husband, he spoke like many conservative Muslims. In short, if the various elements that seem to define a Muslim culture, taken one by one, do not pose the same problems to different European countries, then what is at work in the mirror concepts of Muslim culture and Western culture?

If we want to think about the place of Islam in Europe, we must therefore go beyond narrow consideration of *laïcité à la française*, which is nothing but an exception in Europe itself, and confront the underlying question of the compatibility of Islam with Western secularism.

2

ISLAM AND SECULARIZATION

The improper uses of *laïcité* in contemporary France do not relieve us from the need to confront the underlying question of the relationship among dogma, religious history, and secularization. That there is a specifically Christian element in the history of the construction of the state and of secularization in the West is obvious. The question is to determine whether this model is universally valid, that is, whether, lacking the experience of the institutions that the West has known, real secularization is possible; the second problem is to determine whether other forms of attaining secularization have been experienced in Islam; finally, we have to investigate whether, even in the absence of any real internal process of secularization, it is possible to borrow forms developed elsewhere or whether secularization requires a reformation of Islam.

Is *Laïcité* Christian?

What is specific to Islam, and what is applicable to any religion, at least the major Western monotheistic religions? Many criticisms directed toward Islam are, in fact, in no way particular to it. There are no *laïc* religions, at least not among major revealed monotheistic religions. By definition, a revealed monotheistic religion claims to speak the truth, to have something to say about all human actions and conduct. As Cardinal Ratzinger always maintained when he was head of the Congregation for the Doctrine of the Faith, there is in fact *one* truth.[1] Every believer thinks that God's law is superior to human law and that a parliamentary majority cannot decide what is true: the Catholic Church has never accepted legislation authorizing abortion. *Laïcité* in this sense does not have to do with shared values but, as I have noted, with the acceptance of shared rules of the game, which is not the same thing. Here, it means that the church has rejected violent or illegal forms of opposition to legislation that it nonetheless considers unacceptable. However, even though *laïcité* is now politically accepted, many Christian and Jewish religious dignitaries have alluded to its limits: Archbishop Lustiger, Pastor de Clermont, and Chief Rabbi Josef Sitruk have all protested against the law "on *laïcité*" (the prohibition on students wearing the veil in school) and have not hidden their discomfort at the strengthening of measures excluding religious signs from the public square.[2] The idea that religion cannot be confined to the private sphere is shared by all major religions.

Nevertheless, when the aim is to point to the specific nature of Islam, the emphasis is placed on the fact that Christianity has accepted the principle of *laïcité* (because, as Jesus says in the Gospel, "Render therefore unto Caesar the things which are Caesar's; and unto God the things that are God's" [Matthew 22:21]). But this is to commit the methodological error that has probably most polluted the debate: to move constantly from the theological level to the level of political or even religious practice. When a theologian or a pope refers to Matthew in blessing *laïcité*, there is nothing more Catholic, but the existence of the verse has never guaranteed either secular practice or a theology of *laïcité*. The *Syllabus* written by Pope Pius IX in 1864 expresses a total rejection of *laïcité* as we understand it today (proposition 55 identified by the pope as an erroneous statement: "The Church should be separated from the State and the State from the Church"). When the church finally accepted the secular republic, this was not because a commission of theologians had spent years rereading the Gospels but because the Vatican drew the political lessons from the inescapable advent of the republic and adapted to it (commissions serve only to provide philosophical arguments to justify decisions already made for political reasons). Monsignor Lavigerie's toast to the republic in Algiers in 1890, which signaled the Vatican's acceptance of the republic, was not the work of a theologian but the act of a true politician. The fact that thereafter, with the establishment of Christian Democracy, the majority of the Catholic electorate and clergy entered into the realm of *laïcité* is a good thing that has more to do with social developments and the political practice of believers than with the reference to Matthew. The acceptance of *laïcité* finally had consequences for the political participation of Catholics (Christian Democracy), the presence of the church in the world (Catholic movements such as the Jeunesse Ouvrière chrétienne [Young Christian Workers]), and ecclesiology (worker priests, the nature of the priesthood, the role of the laity), as well as for theology (liberation theology, humanism, and so on). Vatican II was a consequence of the changes brought about by secularization and *laïcité* and embodied an attempt to respond in a positive, coherent, and global way, even if that induced a conservative reaction that in any event, apart from the reactionary supporters of Monsignor Lefebvre, could not undo the past but merely look at it with different eyes. The connection between internal changes in the church and secularization was made after the fact: theological reform is not a condition for the acceptance of *laïcité*. As for secularization, it is happening in any event, even if it may often be deplored.

But this reasoning is not enough to put Islam and Christianity in the same boat; it simply shows that it was not the church that fostered *laïcité* but that the resistance it offered was based on political reasons, in a conflict over power legitimated by theological references. The question is to determine whether the conflict between the church and the modern world could have been resolved following a defeat of Catholic thought in open warfare or whether Christianity did not contain the premises of a theology accepting a dual register: the two kingdoms, earthly and heavenly. Which would amount to saying that political pressure returned the church to the truth of a Gospel message that it had forgotten in its fascination, if not with the exercise of secular power itself, at least with control over it. Did Christianity, despite itself and despite the church, not help to establish the domain of secularization and *laïcité* that we know today?

Marcel Gauchet defines Christianity as the "religion of the exit from religion,"[3] which means not that the church accepted or even supported the secularization of society but that the theological matrix of Christianity allowed for secularization by postulating a center of transcendent power, the state, on the basis of which society could be thought of in nonreligious terms. Secularization does not mean the end of transcendence but the establishment of a nontheological transcendence, in a sense of a secularized religion. It was indeed by going through the sanctification of the state (because it was sanctioned by God) that a certain form of Christianity was able to help legitimate the autonomy of the political sphere. It was Christian writers who theorized the separation of church and state in the Middle Ages, as well as the autonomy of the political and its possible right to control the religious sphere. When William of Ockham (ca. 1285–1349) justified the control of the state over the church, he did so not as a member of the laity (he was a monk) but because he saw in the sovereign an expression of divine will. Law is first of all an expression of will: positive law, the law of the state, does not need to reflect any supposed natural morality; it is foundational, just as the divine will is creative. Hence it was not just the theory of the two kingdoms but the patterning of the earthly kingdom on the heavenly kingdom that made it, in turn, possible to marginalize the religious sphere, because what was secularized was in fact the divine itself. The political space of the West was born out of a Christian religious matrix, the new autonomy of which was theorized against the church as an institution, but by thinkers and agents who were themselves Christians, such as the jurists who patiently defined a state of laws starting from the patrimonial state of the actual sovereign while also recovering the tradition of Roman law. The debate between the two orders arose within the realm of Christian thought. In short, while *laïcité* bars the state from getting involved in dogma, we nonetheless have to raise the question of the religious origins of *laïcité*, origins that in fact frequently reappear. We can push the argument further: the sanctification of the state enabled it to cast the church outside the political realm. The sacred status of the state and its legal order, in this view, are the transposition in the temporal realm of a transcendence defined by religion. The consequence is that there is no true *laïcité* without a strong state: the political domain is at the heart of the process of secularization.

It can thus be said both that *laïcité* was constructed against the Catholic Church (about which historically there is no doubt) and that Christianity made *laïcité* possible. In this sense, we can assert that Protestantism is more modern because, by rejecting the concept of an institutionalized church, it removed the political obstacle to secularization.

Even if we accept the Christian origins of the modern state (and for countries in the Roman law tradition, this seems established fact), that raises several questions: Is passage through the modern transcendent state a necessary condition for the establishment of an autonomous order of the political? Does the fact that a given model arose in a precise religious and historical context make it thereby specific and not exportable to other cultural realms? How does the connection between the order of the religious and the order of the political operate?

41

Is Muslim Dogma an Obstacle to *Laïcité*?

Defining Islam, or any religion, as a precise body of dogmas presupposes a choice both of texts and of interpretations. Any critic of Koranic theology sets himself up as a theologian and thereby enters into the field of his own critique. I will not enter this theological debate, except to make two remarks. First, to define Islam as a body of closed norms and Muslims as making up a community excluding membership in any other group is precisely to adopt the fundamentalists' definition of Islam. This is a reference to an imaginary Islam, not to the real Muslim world, and the fundamentalists are made into authentic representatives of Islam, even if this means speaking with benevolent condescension about the poor liberals who cannot make themselves heard. This is also the source of the exasperation with modern fundamentalists, such as Tariq Ramadan, accused of dual language precisely because they translate this fundamentalism into modern discourse. But at the same time, since talk about dogma is part of the debate, we have to take it into account.

There are, broadly speaking, two opposing schools in contemporary polemics about Muslim dogma. First, there are those who think that Islamic dogma is fundamentally an obstacle to secularization, as it is to the establishment of *laïcité*. The arguments are familiar and circle around three points:

1. In Islam, there is no separation between religion and the state (*din wa dawlat*).
2. Sharia is incompatible with human rights (particularly women's rights) and with democracy (because the law of God is imposed on man).
3. The believer can identify with only the community of believers (*umma*) and hence has no knowledge of the political society of citizens (except to think of the other—that is, the non-Muslim—as a *dhimmi*, or protégé).[4]

Two conclusions are possible: either a theological reformation is necessary, or Islam is not reformable and hence Muslims are definitively barred from modernity as Muslims. This second view is supported by most Islamic fundamentalist movements, which in fact believe, on the one hand, that Islam is a totalizing and inclusive system and, on the other, that it is inviolable, not only with regard to dogma and sharia (that is, general principles) but also in the *fiqh* (concrete application of sharia).

In both cases, we are dealing with what I would call the essentialist position, consisting of seeing in Islam a fixed and timeless system of thought. Critics of Islam and Muslim fundamentalists are mirrors of each other, and each corroborates the other in the view of Islam that they share, merely with the signs reversed. This position is, of course, supported by the paradigm of revelation in Islam: it took place following a noteworthy unity of time (twenty-three years), of place (Mecca and Medina), and of agent (the Prophet Muhammad), unknown to the two other Abrahamic religions.

Countering this approach are reformist, liberal, or simply moderate Muslim thinkers and theologians, who rely on the abundant theological and philosophical debates in Islam at the time of the Umayyad (661–750) and Abbasid (750–1258) dynasties—for example, the rationalist Mutazilite school (whereas, by definition, fundamentalists think of this period as the one when Islam was corrupted by Greek philosophy). These thinkers are, of course, spread over a wide range of opinions, ranging from conservative moderates, theologically very orthodox but very flexible with regard to the possible consequences of dogma in political, social, and cultural fields, to real reformers, who think that the theological question must be reexamined.

Orthodox liberals use the classic techniques of exegesis and jurisprudence (*tafsir* and *hadith* [interpretation of the text and quotations of the sayings and deeds of the Prophet]) and the tools developed by the major legal schools (reasoning by analogy, consensus of scholars, reference to the public welfare, objection to anything

that might create a *fitna* [dissension among Muslims], and so on).
They have a body of references much larger than that of the fundamentalists, who stick strictly to the corpus of the Koran and the
Sunna (*hadith*), but they do not call into question the validity of
that corpus. From the same texts, they derive different conclusions,
obviously much more open than those of the fundamentalists. They
have, for example, challenged the indiscriminate call for jihad, or
for revolt against the established government, even if that government is neither Islamic nor even Muslim. They do not necessarily
adhere to so-called Western values, but they do not systematically
pose the question of the Islamic character of those values. In a
word, everything that is not explicitly against Islam is acceptable.
Renunciation of the idea that there is a specifically Islamic political
form is taken for granted.[5]

This school is, of course, not very dynamic (although some writers, such as the Syrian Sheik Bouti, have developed original thinking on bioethics in the light of Islam). It involves passively absorbing an imposed modernity by declaring it not contrary to Islam but
not giving it an Islamic character or attributing value to it. This
school goes along with secularization, ratifies *laïcité*, but it does
not promote a new religious approach. In this category are found
all the court clerics, muftis of the republic, and imams of the great
official mosques, from Turkey to Morocco, from Paris to Cairo.

Another approach consists of relying on a certain form of casuistry that enables the development of a de facto compromise while
preserving principles: This is the approach, for example, of the
Conseil Européen de la Fatwa (European Council of the Fatwa),
coming, like the Union des organisations islamiques de France,
from Muslim Brotherhood roots, based in London, which defends
the concept of a "*fiqh* of the minority"—that is, a jurisprudence
specific to Muslims living as a minority that would authorize exemptions from a certain number of rules (for example, allowing a
bank loan for the purchase of a house). Another form of this de
facto but not de jure secularization is the position of Tariq Rama-

dan on the moratorium affecting corporal punishment: the norm is not abolished, but it is not practiced. In neither case is it a matter of reformism but rather a practical adaptation that amounts to accepting de facto secularization, hence dissociating religion, society, and politics. An approach of this kind maintains orthodoxy while enabling the believer to live in a society governed by *laïcité*. This is a practical response that dissociates the ideal from the real. But, more deeply, it clearly signals a renunciation of establishing the ideal in the real, even though one may dream of the day when Islam will appear as the solution for the majority of the people. We have survived other varieties of millenarianism.

Reformism in Theology

In parallel with these empirical improvisations, there has appeared a new and truly reformist school, which refuses to enter into the casuistry of the ulema, moderate or fundamentalist. These new theologians (in Iran, they speak of *kalam-i no*, or new theology) have often broken with the traditional ulema and rarely come from madrasas (many of them have had a secular and often a scientific education). The common point among reformists is the idea that the message of the Koran must be separated from its concrete embodiment in a given history and place. For them, jurisprudence (*fiqh*) was constructed on patriarchal cultures and gave shape to a sharia that had at the outset been much more open and various. Islam has to be separated from culture (the Iranians have no hesitation in saying "de-Arabized") and not adapted to a new one. This is the position of new theologians such as Arkun, Soruch, Kadivar, Abu Fadl, and Abu Zayd.[6] Sharia is presented as the matrix of a meaning that the traditional ulema later fossilized into rigid law (*fiqh*). That range of meaning must therefore be reopened, and we must be wary both of particular cultures and of being captured by the established authorities. Government power is not seen as a defender of Islam but, on the contrary, as the origin of its fossilization, because it instrumentalized Islam to perpetuate the established order: democratization thus goes hand in hand with theological openness. Reformism assumes the separation of the political from the religious, less to save politics from religion (as in France) than to save religion from politics and restore freedom to the theologian and the simple believer alike. *Laïcité* is in this view neither the conclusion of a theological argument nor an affirmation of the supremacy in law of secular authority but a methodological principle to improve ways of rethinking religion. Islam has to be disentangled from politics.

The Iranian Abdul Karim Soruch therefore logically defends the need for what he calls the "contraction of religion" (*qabz-e din*), which is in fact a withdrawal of religion from the political sphere but also from traditional society, where it serves primarily to justify social conservatism. The state must be separated from religion: this is indeed a politically *laïque* position. But in this instance *laïcité* precedes secularism. Soruch, like many American Protestants, defends the separation of church and state but wants civil society to remain a religious society. He therefore is reluctant to use the term "secularization": he thinks religion can still play a role in society, which he defines as "religious civil society" (*jame'e-ye madani-ye dini*), an interesting example of *laïcité* without secularization, recalling the program of the American Puritans. Religion here is on the side of resistance to the institutionalization of power: it is not the state that liberates the citizen from religion, as in the French *laïque* tradition, but religion that liberates the citizen from the omnipotence of the state.[7] But how is it then possible to reconcile religious civil society and democracy, since the believer relies on a divine norm? We have to assume that a citizen will act as a believing person, but inwardly, with no coercion emanating either from the state or from a clergy but also without imposing on others what he considers to be the divine norm: the absolute character of faith goes hand in hand with the pluralism of opinions, which means that if a majority of citizens stop conducting themselves as believers, then society has been definitively secularized, because there is no authority to impose faith on the citizen.

This view may be compared with the Calvinist conception of the Puritans, in which the polity (the city-state of Geneva or Boston) is in fact managed by the citizens as a body, with no specifically religious institution seizing control of the state. This lack of institutionalization means that, when the process of the decline not of faith but of the millenarian illusion gets under way, we find ourselves in fact in a secularized democratic world (where some laws, such as the prohibition of adultery, may linger on). Soruch very logically advocates the abolition of the clerical safeguards contained in the constitution of Islamic Iran (the concept of *vilayat-i faqih* [regency of the doctor of the law], which defines the position of the Guide of the Revolution, as well as the Council of Guardians, charged with verifying the Islamic character of laws and electoral candidates, which amounts to censoring the popular will). This is also, interestingly enough, the perspective adopted by the elements grouped together as the Christian Right in the United States, which, however dogmatic it may be, sees elections as the sole source of political legitimacy. The fact that this religious view, designating a liberal in Iran and a conservative in the United States, is the antithesis of French philosophical *laïcité* is beyond question, and it shows that that philosophy holds no monopoly on the establishment of a democratic arena.

Other reformers have opened different paths, since by definition the assertion of the freedom to conduct theological criticism goes hand in hand with pluralism. I will not consider here the diverse analyses of these writers, who, according to Rachid Benzine,

> show that beneath religious discourse there often lie hidden questions and strategies that have to do with culture, anthropology, and political interests. All these thinkers advocate an end to the ideological and practical use of the sacred texts. The Koran has no

authority to answer all contemporary questions. It is neither a legal code nor a treatise on political science. The questions of democracy, *laïcité*, human rights, equality between men and women, must be approached independently of the text of the Koran.[8]

This amounts to making the Prophet a man of his time (which is, in fact, perfectly consonant with the strict monotheism of Islam, for which only God is absolute), rejecting the dogma of the uncreated Koran (which was, in any event, imposed only belatedly by the most rigorous schools like the Hanbali) and therefore using the conceptual tools of modern criticism (linguistics, history, sociology, comparative studies, and so on). It also amounts to turning to reason and personal interpretation, subject to criticism by one's peers.

In every example of this reformism, the legal norm is transformed into an ethical value and can no longer be subject to rigid codification or implemented by the state. The question of the compatibility of sharia with modern law is no longer pertinent, because sharia is no longer defined as a legal code (in fact, the very concept of *fiqh* disappears). Value wins out over the norm, meaning over the word, the spirit over the letter.

This program is very clear, and it is obvious that an Islam of this kind is not only compatible with *laïcité* and secularization but is working toward the latter and justifies the former.

For obvious reasons, I will not consider the question of the acceptability of this reading of Islam. A reformist and liberal Islam exists from the very moment that qualified Muslims set it out in their writings. They are, of course, challenged by other theologians, intellectuals, or activists, but it is not up to Islamologists of court, academy, or cocktail party to distribute good and bad marks from the outside. We simply register the fact that there can be a liberal Muslim theology.

Nevertheless, the problems posed by theological reformism are of two orders: What is its public? Is it a necessary condition for Islam to turn out to be compatible with *laïcité* and democracy?

Presented in those terms, the argument amounts to betting everything on the victory of the liberals over the fundamentalists or else to considering that the liberals have been structurally defeated because they have no audience. It is clear, for reasons I have detailed in *Globalized Islam,* that the forms of religiosity that drive present-day religious revivalism, in all religions, are far from being liberal.[9] The corollary is thus that a forceful policy to foster *laïcité* would lead to promoting this reformist Islam to the detriment of other forms of the religion (fundamentalist, conservative, traditionalist). Once again, the unspoken thought of *laïcité* is indeed interventionism in theology.

But the major problem with this approach is that it gives a privileged place to dogma, without explaining in what way the dogma of a religion is relevant to its relation to the political world and without asking how it operates to produce concrete conduct. The relations among fundamentalism, *laïcité,* and secularization are much more complex (for example, the much-discussed *ijtihad* [right of interpretation] is not in itself a sign of liberalism, since both Saudi Wahhabis and Iranian ayatollahs recognize it, if under supervision). Finally, to undertake a policy of promoting reformist thinkers in the current context, when Muslim identity is tinged with a strongly anti-imperialist hue, would often amount to giving them the kiss of death. It is considered good form in the West to decorate, appoint, and value "good" Muslims, even though it is not clear whether the purpose is to add to their prestige in Muslim countries or, on the contrary, to emphasize their isolation the better to stigmatize the fanaticism and obscurantism of Muslim societies.

A theological reformation makes sense only if it turns on cultural, social, and political issues perceived by those involved. Not all of Martin Luther's ideas were very new, but his stroke of genius was to turn them into a manifesto (ninety-five clear and distinct theses) posted in public, which could circulate because of printing technology and whose political and social implications were immediately understood. In this sense, Luther is closer to Khomeini than to John XXIII. The Islamists have better understood the link between religion and politics than the reformers. Everything suggests that the reformers will have a retroactive influence; that is, they will provide a language in which to think about changes that will have taken place for other reasons.

We therefore also have to look for the roots of secularization in the underlying trends of Muslim societies. The approach of historians and anthropologists consists of investigating the way in which Muslim societies have concretely posed the question of the religious environment in which they exist.

De Facto Forms of *Laïcité*:
History and Societies of the Muslim World

Historians and anthropologists point out that Islam has, in fact, experienced secularization, from both the political and the sociological point of view. The dogma is rich and complex enough to be pulled in different directions; it is also a skillful construction, often very political (largely influenced by history and the choices of monarchs), the diversified development of which opened many paths and fostered debate among enough divergent schools for it to be possible to find what is appropriate. All authorities in Islam were secular in the sense that they were not determined by religious criteria. Except for the period of the Prophet, there was never a theocracy. Sultans, emirs, generals, and presidents took power (and continue to take it) following perfectly temporal processes (force, dynastic succession, coup d'état, or even election) and were content with negotiating their legitimacy with a body of more or less domesticated ulema, to which they conceded control over personal status, reserving positive state law (*qanun*, a Greek word, clearly indicating that the borrowing is acknowledged). The ulema, moreover, developed a whole theory of respect for established authority (including non-Muslim authority), both to guarantee the survival of Muslim society and to avoid *fitna*—that is, the division of the community.[10] A frequently repeated commonplace according to which Islam prohibits Muslims from remaining under a non-Muslim government is false: once again, this depends on the interpreters. It is not an accident that "hard" interpretations, like that of Ibn Taymiyya, are now fashionable in radical Islamic circles, but other equally authorized interpretations exist—for example, in the thought of Tariq Ramadan, which, whatever hesitations it may provoke, is in fact a theory of the legitimacy and practice of a minority Islam. The fact that, for many ulema, this authorization is an expedient or that, for Tariq Ramadan, the ideal would be reached on the day when non-Muslims converted is not a difficulty: the eschatological hope for the triumph of the true religion is inherent in monotheism, Christian or Muslim. The important thing is the definition of a rule of the game respected by everyone in the temporal realm. Everyone is free to dream of revolution, the abolition of capitalism, the coming of the Mahdi or of Christ on earth. Whether you live as an owner of the world or merely as a tenant, the important thing is to respect the terms of the lease.

This political secularity also finds an echo in the strength of nonreligious social structures in Muslim societies. Traditional societies, whatever the validity of the term, are organized according to anthropological rationales (tribalism [*asabiyya*], that is, any form of group solidarity based on consanguinity and marriage connections), codes of behavior, and customary laws in which Islam plays a small role. In southern Egypt, cradle of the radical Gama Islamiya, the *thar*, or traditional vendetta, claims many more victims than does religious violence and is practiced identically among Coptic Christians and Muslims; the appeal to sharia has never managed to do away with it. The Taliban in Afghanistan never managed to replace the tribal code of the Pashtun tribes from which they came (*pashtunwali*) with sharia, whose values are very different (contrary to what is often said, it is not certain that the tribal code is more favorable to women, because it bars their inheriting, requires that a childless widow marry her dead husband's brother, and uses women as a medium of exchange to end vendettas). The colonial powers, from French Morocco to British India, clearly saw and used the anti-Islamic possibilities of custom. Finally, Islam spread through very varied geographical areas, which implies a very wide diversification of Muslim societies (including variations in the status of women); it is possible to speak of varieties of cultural Islam, which demonstrates its great capacity to adapt to different cultures and political systems but also shows that Islam in itself is never the explanation for a social reality.[11]

Full application of a sharia caught between customary law and positive law was never anything but an ideal, or even a political slogan, which incidentally explains why the various fundamentalist groups have been primarily opposition movements. But the way in which sharia is produced, even if its application is in fact limited, also shows that it tends precisely to emancipate itself from political authorities: produced by a body of specialists, following rules that vary from one school to another but that are all based on casuistry, deduction, analogy, and the like, by definition it never takes into consideration the will of the sovereign. By postulating the existence of an autonomous legal space, sharia paradoxically strengthens the autonomy of the political sphere. The tradition of the ulema comes closer to defining a form of civil society than of theocracy, because it escapes from central state control, as long as it does not interfere with the state's prerogatives.

As Olivier Carré points out, if Islam is also concerned with the temporal world, this is because it is affected by that world: the sovereign intervenes much more in religion than the converse; ulema are easily domesticated, scholarship corrected, and censorship applied.[12] The relationship goes in both directions, as quietist Iranian religious figures understood when they asked for a separation of state and clergy: the absence of a distinction between state and religion secularizes religion more than it makes politics religious.

Until the contemporary period, secularization in Muslim countries had taken place routinely, with no tension between secular and religious authorities (except in Iran in the twentieth century, but precisely because Iran has a form of church that does not exist in the Sunni world). In western Europe, conversely, the very nature of power was shaped by that tension. In this sense, Islam never had a theocratic ideal, neither in terms of institutions (the clergy before Khomeini never demanded power) nor even in terms of law: the possible institution of sharia as state law does not in itself define an Islamic state, as all advocates of political Islam have said, from Saïd Qutb to Khomeini.

De facto secularization has also affected Muslim populations, but there has been a refusal to apply to Islam the basic principles of the sociology of religion, which is concerned with the concrete conduct of the believer. This sociology arose from the study of the Christian populations of Europe, and it showed how the changes in the conduct of believers (among other things, the phenomena of de-Christianization) had nothing to do with changes in dogma: the reasons religious observance declined in Beauce but remained constant in Rouergue had nothing to do with theological debate. The same thing is true of Islam: there is an entire realm and process of secularization that has nothing to do with changes in dogma. Of course, the fascinating and complex question remains as to the relationship between theological debate and the sociology of social actors—for example, between the capitalist ethic and Protestantism (Max Weber), between family structure and predestination (Emmanuel Todd).[13] But one thing is certain: there is never any causality (Protestantism creating capitalism, or capitalism giving rise to the Reformation).[14]

Once again, reference to the diversity and secularization of real Muslim societies does not completely resolve the problem, even if it shows that there is a de facto compatibility among Islam, secularization, and *laïcité*. For this diversity and this history have been challenged by political Islamism and the modern forms of fundamentalism. Islamism, which turns Islam into a political ideology, contests the fact that there was ever a truly Islamic state and takes up a modern analysis of the state to try once again to theorize the absence of separation between the religious and the political on the basis of an ideological agent. We are brought back to the question of the state.

Laïcité: Offspring of the Divorce of Church and State

Laïcité in the West was built, above all, on a confrontation between the emperor and the pope, the king and Rome, the republic and the church—that is, between two institutions. The American counter-example is not really to the contrary: it was against the established status of the Church of England they had fled that the Founding Fathers decreed the separation of church and state, which in no way meant a separation of religion from politics (because of the importance of civil religion). Hence the American form of separation was put into place in response to a European complex of problems.

The question of *laïcité* in the Western world is not so much one of the relationship between the sacred and the profane, because in the end both fields lay claim to the same sense of the sacred. *Laïcité à la française* was unable to find a footing in the Muslim world for lack of the two agents that engendered it: a sanctified state and an ecclesiastic institution in competition not for temporal power but for the hierarchical organization of the temporal world according to the terms of a sacred space. This explains why when Mustafa Kemal Atatürk imported the Jacobin state into Turkey, along with all its apparatus of legitimacy (nationalism, school, myth of the unitary nation), he had no need to exclude the clergy, because they did not constitute another center of legitimacy: he merely turned them into state employees.

Moreover, the institution and sanctification of the Western state are, as I have discussed, inseparable from the state's assumption of a religious matrix in order to establish itself. Law is founded on the will: of God, of the sovereign, of the political body. Particular or general, the will is sacred. In this case, the state is the bearer of values: republican values are positive. The combat between church and state is stronger (even when both share the same faith) the more they rely on the same image of legitimacy, an identical space for the construction of society. At bottom, there is no *laïcité* without a strong state. As I have mentioned, it was in fact the sanctification of the state that made possible the emergence of a secular space. Religion is here the condition for secularism, by its passage through the realm of politics.

In Sunni Islam, there is neither church nor sanctification of the state. Power is contractual, not because of the will of the people but because it is contingent: the sultan or the emir takes power by force and keeps it by a more or less explicit contract with the ulema (as long as he defends Islam abroad and advocates sharia domestically, he is legitimate); victory or defeat is the sign of only divine approval or divine indifference. Power is never transcendent or sacred. Neither is it the source of *the* law. The state in Islam has always been weak, less for the reasons given by Montesquieu (despotism of a single man) than, on the contrary, because civil society enjoyed resilience made stronger by two phenomena: *asabiyya* and sharia. Strong power does not mean a strong state.

But if the state and *laïcité* are thus closely associated, Islam would have to go through the experience of the modern strong state, and not the despot. Democracy would be possible only after the establishment of a modern state. This is why there is constant discussion of the Turkish model. Islam is said to have missed history's train, and, for many, only a harsh pedagogy can enable it to catch up on all the stages, which justifies both certain forms of colonialism (protectorate, for example) and support of secular authoritarian regimes (President Ben Ali in Tunisia) and military interventions leading to more or less lengthy periods of supervision (Iraq after the 2003 American intervention).[15]

The discussion then shifts from secularization to the question of the state, which is not at all surprising, since we have seen the extent to which, in the European and especially the French tradition, any reflection about democracy and *laïcité* is inseparable from the question of the state. Does the fact that a paradigm is the product of a particular history mean that it does not have universal value? Or do the historical conditions that produced it have to be repeated (speeded up and hence giving rise to violence and misunderstanding) for it to be adopted?

The Political Imagination of Islam: Is There a Muslim Political Culture?

Far from tracing a continuity over fourteen centuries of history, Islam is very flexible, establishes no *ex ante* model, and adapts to different political systems. The systematic reference to a Muslim political culture, however, suggests that there is an invariant, imaginary configuration of power that structures the relationship of the Muslim with the political realm and is now resurfacing in the difficulty of integrating the model of the modern state and democracy.

How can we think of the return of the religious otherwise than as a form of archaism? Archaism presumes the persistence of a way of thinking, momentarily masked by modernity but returning like a founding repressed element, like the truth of an identity in search of itself. The attempt is always made to define in these terms a religious invariant, dogma, mentality, or culture that would explain the different answers each society provides to the questions of social order, political forms, economic practices, the relationship to space, and the definition of the self.

The underlying problem remains the same: How does a religion operate in the social and political realms? How does it determine the conduct of believers? One can, of course, reason in terms of mentality: the believer has internalized the norm according to which there is no difference between state and religion; hence he cannot manage to adapt to *laïcité*. But why would the believer have internalized that norm and not another? What is the relationship between a norm and a practice? Did the Christian prohibition of adultery diminish the number of times it was committed in the Christian world? Certainly not, even though it helped to create a market of guilt, which was handled, moreover, with a great variety of responses and devices. The norm is thus not innocent, but it never operates directly.

A religious norm functions as a social or political norm only because it is adopted, reformulated, and expressed by mechanisms that all presuppose the intervention of other authorities (and other systems of norms): law and the political order but also forms of religiosity that vary over time and space. Dogma exists only through rereading and implementation—that is, in a form of religiosity. In this book, I have developed my view that the principal agent in the establishment of what is known as *laïcité* was the political order, not dogma. *Laïcité* is established by political means, and that holds for Islam, whereas secularization is instituted by changes in the believer's forms of religiosity.

It is therefore very important to see how religious conceptions are expressed with respect to integration into the world, social program, and relationships to society and territory. What counts for us is not the content of dogma in itself but its formulation in relation to the believer's integration into the world. This integration is not abstract. Even if the believer considers himself the guardian of a faith and a vision of salvation that is valid in every time and place, it is obvious that he expresses it in a particular context. It is impossible to understand anything, for example, of theological disputes at particular moments in history (say, the fifth and sixteenth centuries for Christianity) if they are considered to be timeless.

It is possible, of course, to speak of a political imagined world of Islam—that is, of recurring theories of power among ulema and thinkers—but what is striking is that they are never put into operation. They have never helped define a type of political system, except when they left the juridical realm to move into that of ideology (Khomeini), and this is a modern phenomenon. What dogma defines is not a political system but a political imaginative vision, which of course depends on interpretation. The dominant political vision today, among Islamists as well as neofundamentalists, is that of the time of the Prophet. But this political vision is not a transmission of the past (why would it have taken Muslims fourteen centuries to notice that only the Prophet's model of the polity is legitimate?). Bringing up to date the originating past is, as so often, an attempt to appropriate a form of modernity.

Take the example of the constant confusion of Islamists with neofundamentalists.[16] For the former, re-Islamization will come through the state; for the latter, through personal piety. They all nevertheless share the same political vision: the idea that the ideal Muslim society is the one that existed at the time of the Prophet. But this paradigm never operates directly. Many ulema and more modern writers have spent pages defining the conditions required to become a caliph, but no one has ever seriously gone in search of that caliph: the theme has now been taken up by political sects (like Hizb-ut-Tahrir, a semiclandestine party now established in London that recruits among young Muslims of the second generation), following a rationale that no longer has anything to do with traditional Islamic law (the caliphate of Hizb-ut-Tahrir is embodied in fact by the party itself, not by an individual: this conception of the party as a political actor in itself is a legacy of Marxism).[17]

If one may, in fact, establish a list of what would make up the foundation of Islamic political vision (the caliphate, the absence of separation of religion and politics), it can be seen that these paradigms operate through the intermediary of a legal or an ideological elaboration. A religious dogma never has a direct effect in politics. It operates only if it is adopted, expressed, and redefined by a political ideology, a legal elaboration, or a mechanism of power, all of which depend on a precise political situation (we shall see how the Islamic state is, in fact, an ideological elaboration specific to the twentieth century).

But some writers, such as Samuel Huntington (and dominant opinion), envisage a direct link between dogma and political system, a link supposedly materialized by a culture: Muslim or Arab-Muslim culture. In short, even if it is thought that Muslim societies are subject to a process of secularization, Islam nevertheless marks their political culture and indeed the cast of mind of individual agents, just as secularized Europe remains deeply Christian. The holistic vision of Islam is thus thought to survive in the political ideologies of the Middle East (with pan-Arabism merely the secularization of pan-Islamism), and the difficulty of thinking about autonomous political institutions and of conceiving of the citizen independently of his clan ties or his affective fusion with the community are seen as the sign of the persistence of an Arab-Muslim culture stubbornly resistant to the establishment of the modern state.

From the outset, I have reiterated the same question: What allows us to say that dogma determines the conduct of believers? For fundamentalists and born-again Christians, the answer seems obvious: the believer himself decides to put forward the prescriptions of dogma. For a Muslim identified sociologically, one who does not feel the need to set forth his faith explicitly, we turn to the concept of culture, which is supposed, in addition, to operate to explain why a society is determined by religion, although that religion is explicit nowhere in either law or institutions.

In short, culture is seen as the agent that enables religion to shape a society and also to shape a mentality. This is the underlying concept behind the notion of the "clash of civilizations": civilizations are in essence religious, even when they are secularized. One cannot escape from religion, and culture is the mediator between religion and society: it is what is left of religion when faith is lost. Secularization is therefore the persistence of the religious phenomenon without the sacred. This is consonant with analyses that consider French *laïcité* to be an inverted form of religious transcendence.

There are thus two scenarios that confine Islam to its insularity: secularized religion expressed in culture and fundamentalist religion expressed directly in the demand for theocracy. Even when one no longer believes, one remains a Muslim. The fear of communitarianism is more easily understood, because the Muslim sociologically defined thereby becomes by definition permeable to any religious reactivation of the culture of religious origin that he bears within: fundamentalism is thus always seen as an extension of the culture of origin. True *laïcité* would then require the renunciation of any referent for identity other than political citizenship.

The problem with the kind of analysis that claims to explain culture by means of religion is that the founding religious element can never be isolated as such: the so-called Arab-Muslim culture derives, in fact, more from the anthropology of Arab societies than from Islam in itself. It introduces a false continuity (from pan-Islamism to pan-Arabism) that leaves borrowings out of account (for example, pan-Arabism is a form of ethnic nationalism, on the model of the pan-Germanism earlier developed in Europe; similarly, the Islamic state derives from a modern vision of the ideological state). In fact, Muslim culture is an imaginary construction made up of elements of dogma, historical paradigms, sociological characteristics, and ways of thinking, all unified under the name of culture. The term "culture" is redundant: Islamic or Muslim culture is presented as the invariant in every possible variety of Muslin society. You generally find in it only what you have put there in the first place. Besides, even if cultures have a religious basis (I will not discuss that point here), some paradigms (like the state or democracy) can very well become autonomous and be exported: the question, then, is whether a political model can be implanted in a new context, and there are no grounds for assuming incompatibility. But we still have to determine whether the acquisition of this new model presupposes going through the historical sequence that brought it into being. The context of deterritorialization (immigration, for example) has dissociated the political models used from their cultures of origin. The great mistake of the use of culture as a basis for social analysis, with respect to the religious question, is that it sees fundamentalism as the reactivation of the religious dimension of a traditional culture, whereas modern fundamentalists are, on the contrary, participants in a process of the loss of cultural identity. It is the return of the religious that calls into question the link between culture and religion, in a way that is perhaps more radical than the slow processes of secularization.

It is indeed the question of globalization that is at issue in every case: the universalization of legal and political models and/or the universalization of modes of religiosity relatively independent of the theological content of religions. I have referred to the debate about Protestantism and capitalism: we can see very clearly how a new work ethic was established in the framework of capitalism but also how it was exported not only to Catholics but to Muslims (for example, in the form of the Müsiad, a Turkish syndicate bringing together small enterprises strongly imbued with a work ethic).[18]

The question then becomes to determine whether these two forms of globalization come together, whether, contrary to the rather provincial view of French universalism, the development of new models of state and society (specifically civil society) and the development of individualistic and culturally unattached forms of fundamentalism do not go hand in hand. In a word, globalization may foster the development of religious fundamentalism while weakening the kind of state that made *laïcité* possible. And this is probably what is happening.

A subsidiary question is to find out whether this is desirable. But to answer otherwise than by pious *laïque* hopes, we have to examine the dynamic processes in operation.

The Parenthesis of the Islamic State
and the Establishment of a Space for *Laïcité*

The entire history of the Muslim world shows that power was, in fact, secular and never sanctified. And it is the re-Islamization in the twentieth century that has called into question the balance between politics and religion, by means of a rereading of Islam (Islamism, neofundamentalism) that obviously presents itself as a return to the sources but is in reality an ideological inflection of religion. When they insist on the need to return to the time of the Prophet, Islamists and neofundamentalists alike are the first to say that no political formation in the Muslim world ever corresponded to a true Islamic state. The question of the state is, indeed, a very modern question.

It was constituted on the basis of two models. The first is the adoption of a secular and authoritarian state apparatus of a European type, following the model of enlightened despotism in the nineteenth century (Muhammad Ali in Egypt), then with Mustafa Kemal Atatürk and Reza Shah in the twentieth, in the form of regimes of a socialist or fascist type (single party, charismatic leader, large role for the security services and the army), from Nasserism to the Algerian Front de libération nationale to Baathism. These models of authoritarian *laïcité* were never able to incorporate democracy, except in Turkey. The second model is the Islamic state, the product in fact of a transformation of Islam into a political ideology, largely under the influence of European political philosophies in which it is the state that shapes society.

In the case of authoritarian secular states, the popular demand for an Islamic state appears precisely as a protest and a quest for authenticity on the part of society, especially when these states have lost their anti-imperialist and nationalist legitimacy (Egypt after Nasser, Algeria after Boumediene). The rejection of *laïcité* is a rejection of the regime and the hope that any future regime will be under the control of a law beyond that of men and will hence exclude corruption and personal power. This is not a matter of the protest of a traditional society but, on the contrary, the expression of a desire to reappropriate the state by a new generation arising out of state transformation: students, urban populations, technocrats.

I have already studied the aporia of the Islamic state.[19] Suffice it to say that its definition, by Abul Ala Maududi, Khomeini, or the Muslim Brotherhood, is not drawn from sharia or the political traditions of the Muslim world but represents, in fact, an Islamic reading of modern political concepts (state, revolution, ideology, society), hence precisely a reflection on the autonomy and prevalence of the political sphere, using ideology as a mediating concept: the Islamic state is not only a state that recognizes sharia as state law but one that makes religion a state ideology. In a state of that kind, like Islamic Iran, religion does not define the place of politics but the converse. The only place where an Islamic state has been instituted is Iran, and this is probably not an accident because the country contains the two power centers: church and state. Moreover, it has been shown how the Islamic revolution in fact helped to further bring society under state control.[20] But, most important, it is starting from this configuration that the question of *laïcité* can really begin to be addressed by considering the separation between the body of producers of knowledge and religious norms and the managers of the state.

The ascendancy of ideology is nothing but the return of politics, the affirmation of the supremacy of the political over traditional religious law. But the effect of an Islamic regime of this kind is always its opposite: accelerated secularization with, for Iran, a decline in religious observance and, for Afghanistan after the defeat of the Taliban, a depoliticization of Islam. Alongside reformers in Iran, traditionalist clerics also call not for secularization (they insist that civil society must be religious) but for separation of church and state, in order to save the church. The position of Ayatollah al-Sistani in Iraq, although it is in line with the constant attitude of the higher

Iraqi Shiite clergy throughout the twentieth century, should also be understood in the light of the failure of the Islamic revolution in Iran: Sistani does not want an Islamic state that would undermine the very foundations of religious legitimacy, and he therefore refuses to get involved in the details of everyday politics.

The question is thus not that of the persistence of an Islamic culture but of the sudden appearance of new ways of religion becoming ideological and of new forms of religiosity in the framework of the modern nation-state.

Islamic revolutions thus lead to the establishment of a de facto *laïcité* because, by excessively politicizing religion, they make it lose its role as a recourse and induce traditional clerics and new believers alike to dream of a spiritual arena outside politics. What then remains in power is no longer a religion but a political-clerical apparatus that uses the moral order to conserve its position of power. In that case, the return of religious feeling takes place beyond politics, outside official religion, indeed outside orthodox Shiite Islam: the return of Sufism, syncretism, interest in Christianity, not to mention, of course, atheism. The politicization of religion ended up by separating religion from politics. The demand for democracy can finally be *laïque*.

3

THE CRISIS OF THE SECULAR STATE AND THE NEW FORMS OF RELIGIOSITY

The Muslim world is, of course, not alone in having been affected by changes in the relationship between religion and politics. We are perhaps witnessing a new configuration of the relations among religion, state, and society, following a model closer to Anglo-Saxon secularization than to French *laïcité*. Religion has, in fact, taken up a position in a society decreasingly under the control of the state. The West is now going through a clear balancing between a demand for a tutelary state, one that protects a national community, and the growth of a philosophy of civil society, where the state is only a somewhat distant arbiter. A balancing, because we are not contrasting two antagonistic categories (for instance, the United States under the Republican Party and the French Jacobin state) but reference points that are invoked in alternation. It is on this terrain of the complex relations among the weakening of the state, supranational organizations, civil society, and the democratization of authoritarian regimes that religious revivalism prospers: as the political arena has grown more complex, the old binary opposition of *laïcité* (state/religion) has found it difficult to incorporate the new forms of religiosity. This is, however, the issue.

Secularization Strengthens the Specificity of Religion

Whereas French *laïcité* was instituted by political choices, secularization in contrast arose from cultural processes that were not decreed, which poses the problem of the relation between explicit religion (dogma and prescriptions) and the internalization of a religious vision of the world in the form of a culture (this religious vision may even be expressed in open unbelief but preserve the intellectual framework of religion, for example, Marxist messianism, secular "saints," pan-Arabism). Secularization is clearly a societal process; that is, it affects a society deeply, although it cannot be assigned to any particular level of that society (the economy, sociology, the role of intellectuals, and so on). It is the way a society looks at the world that changes, although that is not necessarily expressed in an explicit system of thought. We can assume that there can be no *laïcité* unless secularization has come first, but secularization does not necessarily lead to explicit *laïcité*. Secularization by definition affects a society; it is not a system of thought: the secularization of religious behavior has occurred in the Western world without theologians necessarily drawing any conclusions from the process.[1] But secularization automatically brings about a redefinition of religious adhesion (unless we think of it as a mere relic condemned to disappear). Once the religious authorities accept the fact that true believers have become a minority, then the relationship with the "others" has to be reconsidered (until then, they would have been thought of as either sinners or indifferent, while in both cases remaining the concern of the church). But is someone who has been secularized still an unconscious Christian, or is he a pagan who has changed his cultural universe? Secularization brings about a reconstruction of religious identity as a minority identity, except that it may be subsumed in a concept as vague as Judeo-Christian civilization. Having faith or not becomes a criterion of differentiation between two groups. A fairly clear but shifting line can be drawn in Christian churches and Muslim ulema alike between two tendencies, exclusion and co-optation: Who, for example, will be denied a religious funeral, like actors in Europe in the seventeenth century? Secularization brings about the loss of the prominent social presence of religion and the obligation to define oneself explicitly as a believer (or nonbeliever), not because the nonbeliever campaigns against the religious community but because the conditions for belonging to the religious group have become stricter: one's faith must be displayed. The intensification of signs of religious belonging goes hand in hand with the transformation of the group of believers into a minority (not necessarily in terms of numbers: even in societies in which the majority of the population are believers, like the United States, many believers see themselves as members of a cultural minority in an environment that they see as materialist and immoral).

The current revival of religious sentiment makes sense only because it is occurring, in the Muslim world as well, against a background of secularization. It is an expression not of the persistence of religion but of a reorganization of the religious phenomenon according to patterns no longer operating within the traditional framework of the church–state pair. The issue is how to deal with modern forms of fundamentalism much more than how to refurbish an obsolete tool of analysis.

Orphan *Laïcité*

If a compromise on the role of religion was reached in Europe in the course of the twentieth century, this was not only because the various participants came to an agreement on how to share the same political space but also because believers had finally assimilated the definition of religion provided by *laïcité* and had become culturally *laïque*, considering their own observance a private, unostentatious act concerning only the individual person. Political *laïcité* went along with a thoroughgoing secularization of society, including those countries of northern Europe in which the churches maintained their official status: religious observance declined everywhere. But political *laïcité* was largely the result of a compromise between two institutional actors: the state and the church. And both of them are in crisis. The nation-state, although it has not exactly disappeared, has been weakened by globalization and the construction of Europe, while the mechanisms for social integration and social cohesion have also been weakened (school, army, labor market, in parallel with increasing urban segregation). But the churches have also been challenged as institutions, not by the state or by secularization but, on the contrary, by a religious revival that has bypassed them. The new believers may very well accept *laïcité* as the rule of the game in the public square, but they no longer adopt it as a way of living their religion in private. They want to be recognized as religious in the public square. What is at issue, then, is not really a revision of the 1905 law to adapt it to Islam, and there is no challenge to the rules of the game between state and religion; rather, the relation of religion to the public square is no longer seen as being established under the purview of the state. The relationship between religion and politics has become asymmetrical: religious fundamentalism is not interested in political power (even in the United States, except for passing legislation) but in society. This is also true for Muslim neofundamentalism; to argue that the fact that Tariq Ramadan is the heir of the founder of the Muslim Brotherhood means that he has a strategy that is in the final analysis political (an Islamic state in France) is to fail to understand the lack of interest in state institutions that characterizes all contemporary fundamentalist movements: the state in their eyes is not an instrument for the transformation of society; rather, they hold that the return of individuals to faith will make it possible to restore society to a religious foundation. They are in this way surfing the wave of individualism and the prominence of civil society. And this is why the traditional tools of *laïcité* aimed at the juridical definition of the social bond no longer work (even radicals like Bin Laden have no program for a state).

The rise of Islam is contained within a larger phenomenon: for the past twenty years, the West has been experiencing what has been called a religious revival. We should not be deceived by the term: it does not mean an increase in observance but greater visibility for it, and particularly the appearance of so-called fundamentalist forms of religiosity—that is, when the believer refuses to keep his faith private and is determined to have it recognized as an integral part of his public existence, deeming that religion should govern all his personal conduct. Among these movements, we find all forms of charismatic Christianity (Catholics included), Orthodox Judaism, sects (Jehovah's Witnesses), and, of course, Islamic fundamentalism. The qualitative change in the form of observance is more important than the quantitative increase in the number of believers: while young people were eager to meet Pope John Paul II at World Youth Day, enrollments in Catholic seminaries have been in steep decline. The new forms of religiosity are individualistic, very mobile (there are frequent moves from one group to another, even from one religion to another), weakly institutionalized (there is mistrust of churches and representative bodies), anti-intellectual (hence unconcerned with theological articulation), and often communitarian, but in the sense in which one joins a community of believers (and not a community of origin).[2] The community is a choice of belonging and not a cultural heritage.

States have difficulty dealing with what is seen as the revival of religious sentiment with the classic tools of *laïcité* because the ground on which it stands is in crisis. The Jacobin state has been weakened by the development of supranational bodies but also by the emergence of notions like civil society, which is constructed specifically outside the state. Economic liberalism, the construction of globalized and nonterritorial identities (religious identities, in particular), the mobility of individuals, and the flexibility of identity all by definition change the way in which it is possible to think about the revival of religious sentiment. The new forms of religiosity are much better adapted to globalization: I have studied this for Salafism,[3] but it is equally true for all forms of Christian evangelicalism, which have had great success in their proselytism, precisely because they have helped to separate religion from any particular cultural roots and can therefore respond to the needs of populations that have experienced a loss of cultural identity. Conversely, traditional churches (Catholic, Orthodox, Anglican) remain closely tied to particular cultures, sometimes to nation-states (the prevailing case for the Orthodox Church, which is always national), and therefore have much less success in recruiting converts. A religion is all the more fascinating when it is detached from any context, freed of any territory, not to say exotic.[4]

One may, of course, see this development as negative and believe that it should be fought: sovereignists like Jean-Pierre Chevènement are consistent both in their rejection of Europe and in their treatment of religion. This book is not an apology for inevitable globalization. I simply wish to show that the framework of *laïcité* makes it possible to deal with contemporary religious fundamentalism only in coercive ways, for which indeed its defenders have increasingly become the advocates (or, rather, the prosecutors). But the consequence is a serious one, because it consists of dissociating *laïcité* and democracy. We know the old saying "No freedom for the enemies of freedom," but, aside from the fact that this was precisely the slogan that established the Terror, the question really has to do with the effectiveness of such a policy. It was logical for hard-line *laïcs* to support the "eradicators" of the Algerian army against the Islamists. But it is not certain that the result has been democracy or even the establishment of a modern constitutional state in Algeria. My initial hypothesis here is that the appeal to sovereignty is a rearguard battle.

That being said, in France we perhaps have too great a tendency to view the question of globalization solely through the prism of the Jacobin state. It is not the state itself that is in crisis but a certain model of centralized Jacobin nation-state that is the driving force of French society. It is not certain that one may speak, for example, of a model of the Western state that could be contrasted to the weakness of the state in the Muslim world. The model of state building now proposed to developing countries and implemented by the international community in very diverse forms is not the model of the Jacobin nation-state but that of a technocratic state functioning as an arbiter and on a voluntarily reduced scale. One of the most visible elements is the insistence on the privatization of the economy, but the whole technocratic rather than political approach to the construction of the state points in the same direction: institutions (justice, finance) are set up entirely on the basis of the training of competent personnel, whereas social action is entrusted to nongovernmental organizations (NGOs) or United Nations agencies, which by definition have nothing to do with the question of the nation-state. The activity of the Organization for Security and Co-operation in Europe in the former Communist countries, the programs of the United Nations Development Programme and the World Bank, the funding of NGOs by the European Union or the U.S. Congress, not to mention the direct action of occupying powers (the Coalition Provisional Authority in Iraq under Paul Bremer in 2003 and 2004)—all international action has gone to build minimum states and foster transnational institutions. The question of democratization is now addressed through the development of civil society. NGOs, French, British, or American, all work in the same direction, so much so that the French state model has no mechanism by which it can be exported, because all rationales for democratization have been constructed following other models.

Only relics are left of bilateral cooperation centered on government reform of the former colonies.

The sanctification of the state is obvious in countries in the Roman law tradition but not at all in common law countries like the United Kingdom and the United States. The dominant model of the state underlying the democratization process today is the Anglo-American rather than the Continental European model. An entire school of thought, obviously Anglo-American, sees in Protestantism and the common law the true modernity, where it is a contract between individuals that establishes political bonds, with no delegation of authority to a tutelary state and without making the state the embodiment of the popular will: it remains an arbiter and not an autonomous authority.[5] It is clear that the common law had nothing to do originally with Protestantism (another myth of the religious origins of political cultures). Established in medieval England beginning with the Plantagenets—that is, with a French dynasty—it was also developed by monks in the abbeys of a still-Catholic England, but following a logic very different from that of the jurists of the French monarchy. But the conjunction of the two (common law and Protestantism) makes up a coherent whole defining a constitutional state on bases very distant from French Jacobinism. The latest modernity has arrived today with the advent of the concept of civil society.[6] Even though I do not believe for a minute that this civil society—incidentally, rather mythical—has replaced the state, the fact remains that the state model of the Jacobin type is in crisis and that the question of democratization is posed in different terms. We cannot escape from the debate on civil society, communities, group identities, and so forth. Even if we do not support a model of multiculturalism (which is functioning nowhere), we are obliged to take into account what the French Revolution sought to erase: intermediate bodies and coalitions—that is, groups of people who view the individual outside the state, man outside citizenship. In addition, globalization has developed not only transnational, particularly religious, communities but also virtual communities through the Internet, communities that have grown outside the territory of the nation-state. This is no doubt the focus of the dispute between a French and Continental view of the state (the state is the truth of society) and an Anglo-American view where the relationship to the state is contractual and the state is not the bearer of value, apart from the neutral value of tolerance.

In a perspective of democratization of a society where the state is no longer seen (rightly or wrongly) as a building block of society insofar as it provides the society with its political form and where no church defines a corresponding center of legitimacy and power, the notion of *laïcisation* makes no sense. Only secularization counts.

In France, we nevertheless continue to think about secularization in the form of *laïcité* and hence as allegiance to the state. Catholicism has a mediated relationship with the political realm through the intermediary of the church. Islam and Protestantism do not: they are thus in an infrapolitical or overpoliticized state. Being overpoliticized is, of course, a matter of ideology: it is carried out by the mobilization of a theological apparatus, a body of men, as in the Islamic revolution. The real problem in Islam is not *laïcité* (no more than for the Protestant countries of northern Europe, where the Reformation assumed responsibility for eliminating the church as an institution in rivalry with the state) but secularization: in this sense, Islam is in tune with the contemporary issues of secularization.

Contemporary Fundamentalism as an Agent of Globalization

The point held in common by Christian and Islamic fundamentalism is that they strive to define a pure religion divorced from any cultural, social, or anthropological reference and hence, of course, from any national reference (although nationalism resurfaces in its way). Let me recall the principal characteristics I set out in chapter

73

8 of *Globalized Islam.* Neofundamentalism presupposes a break with previous forms of religious observance: it is a religion of the born again. It rejects the cultural and familial heritage and tends to think that existing forms of worship are lukewarm or tinged with paganism. It believes that salvation is attained immediately through faith and hence outside any theological learning: the Taliban were proud of being only students but thought they could teach the doctors of the law a thing or two by the intensity of their piety. Neofundamentalists see in religion a body of dogma, of rites, and of norms defining a code rather than a body of knowledge. Knowledge is immediately accessible ("Everything you need to know about" Islam, Christ, salvation, the Bible—take your pick—in a few lines), and acquiring it seems a kind of revenge against the difficulty of mastering knowledge in school and university (in this sense, the re-Islamization of many young men in France is often linked to a feeling of educational exclusion). The norms are implemented through admonition or by the religious police. Neofundamentalists believe that culture is either redundant (it is the same thing as religion) or threatening (it adulterates the purity of religion): therefore, the fine arts, novels, music (except for religious music), and entertainment are all banned. Neofundamentalists, Muslims and Protestants alike, are not interested in social and economic questions (they are generally economic liberals). They presuppose a social homogeneity (everyone is equal before God) while disregarding social and economic inequalities; the question of the difference between the sexes is, on the contrary, primordial and constitutes the only true social differentiation, to which is added the boundary between believers and unbelievers, since there is no sharing of a nonreligious common culture with one's fellow citizens (here we can see that Catholic conservatism is not fundamentalist, because the church of John Paul II fought specifically to have Europe recognize a common Christian culture shared by believers and nonbelievers).

Making an apologia for the loss of cultural identity as a preliminary condition for the attainment of a pure faith, Christian (essentially Protestant) and Islamic (in the form of Salafism) neofundamentalism affects populations that feel they have been uprooted or have lost their cultural identity or both, and it supplies them with compensation for that loss. *Hallal* fast food and Mecca Cola replace traditional Ottoman or Moroccan cuisine. Neofundamentalism consists of isolating the markers of religious purity (*hallal*) and then superimposing them on a civilization that is seen as solely materialist and instrumental. Neofundamentalism is thus effective in converting and reconverting the faithful. But contrary to what has been said, Islam is not the only proselytizer: while many black Americans have adopted Islam, hundreds of thousands of Latino immigrants from Catholic backgrounds have shifted to Protestantism in the United States. In Brazil, the Universal (Protestant) Church has made huge inroads among Catholics. More interesting in the context of this book, in Central Asia, Baptists, Pentecostals, and Jehovah's Witnesses have converted Muslims by the tens of thousands (in France, the Jehovah's Witnesses have also made inroads among socially dislocated Muslims, such as single mothers from the Maghreb).

Detached from any territory, with no social or economic program, neofundamentalists are not interested in the state, as Sébastien Fath points out, for example, in reference to evangelical movements in the United States.[7] We need to reconsider the whole theory that sees George W. Bush as the representative of a Christian Right that has a political and strategic program. The Christian Right supports Bush so that he will get certain legislation on morality enacted, but it goes no further than that: the real plan for reshaping the Middle East was developed by neoconservatives who are not at all religious. The same thing goes for Islamist neofundamentalists. It is nonsense to assume that Muslim Brothers detached from any territory have a state program: they had one in Egypt (and some still do), but detachment from territory by definition brings about the end of a vision of the state. To accuse Tariq Ramadan (who is not a pure neofundamentalist, because he sees the norm in terms of values, not constraints) of aiming to create an Islamic state in France is absurd.

But the problem lies precisely there: detached from any territory, devoid of cultural identity, and global, neofundamentalism is outside the arena of the state. The state has no grip on it, because the two are in different worlds.

In the conflict between church and state around 1900, there were two adversaries and rivals in competition for similar prizes (in fact, the control of values through the educational system). The church was defending its established position. But today the neofundamentalists ask for nothing positive from the state, except abstention: let us wear the veil, eat *hallal*, not shake hands, and so on. They are absent from the great debates about society because they legislate for themselves, not for society. The church wanted and still wants to impose its values because it believes them to be universal, linked to a natural morality, and expressing the good in general. For neofundamentalists, the law is not the good; it is the law.

By definition, neofundamentalism attracts the uprooted and hence a fringe of second-generation immigrants. But also, and by definition, it finds converts among non-Muslims who feel uprooted (rebels without a cause, racial minorities, young whites from the *banlieues* who have gone through hell with their immigrant pals and been born again).

But while neofundamentalism may not be interested in the issue of *laïcité*, it has not escaped from the question of secularization. Neofundamentalism is a paradoxical agent of secularization, as Protestantism was in its time (although this is far from obvious in reading Calvin), because it individualizes and desocializes religious observance. It addresses the individual who explicitly decides to place his life exclusively under the sign of religion and who for that reason breaks with the majority environment. The individual obviously does not see himself as secular or secularized but, on the contrary, like all the born again, as entirely determined and motivated by religion. But because this relationship with religion isolates him from his social surroundings (or leads him to re-create a communitarian space that amounts to isolation shared with several others), he then draws a line on his own between a sanctified world and the rest of society.[8] This is a configuration that is found in American Protestant fundamentalism as well: a recent work of fiction is built around the distinction between the saved and the "left behind"; one is in or out (the notion of those saved from hell is found in the names of some radical Islamic fundamentalist groups).[9] The return of religious sentiment in the form of sects and communities is merely the homage virtue pays to vice: secularization has won. This is why the tendency to communitarianism, denounced by the advocates of strict *laïcité*, is not a challenge to secularization but a participant in the reconstruction of the division between the two realms.

How to Deal with Neofundamentalism

Neofundamentalism is seen today as a social threat—that is, one more element in the disintegration of the social fabric. This has little to do, however, with the "clash of civilizations." What critics of multiculturalism and communitarianism fail to understand is that the communities reforged by neofundamentalists are not the expression of traditional cultures. Holland was shocked by the assassination of Theo Van Gogh, but although the assassin is of Moroccan origin, he is Dutch, writes in Dutch, and supports a global Islam. He is all the readier to sense that this Islam is in danger because it no longer has territorial boundaries: it is an abstract identity with no roots in a particular society or culture that, in this case, took on concrete form by the act of faith of the believer who drew the border with the thrust of a knife into the neck of the blasphemer. Today's communitarianism is the reconstruction of an imaginary community located in a realm other than that of the nation-state.

For a secular state like France, the first reaction was to restore territoriality in every domain. The first thing was to homogenize public space by banning religious expression, which was confined to another realm. The prohibition of the veil in school appeared as an extension of the battle to drive the Catholic Church out of it, but it is in fact very different: if a priest in his cassock was a competitor for control over the same space, a student wearing a veil is not involved in a struggle for power but rather expressing the abandonment of that public space. The restoration of territoriality also means the quest for a national Islam. This is a logical and desirable approach, as long as it is understood that there can be no question of defining a liberal and acceptable dogma. Indeed, for a policy of the restoration of territoriality to succeed, it must be one that integrates not excludes; that is, it must offer a place to Islam without raising the question of dogma, only that of the rules of the game. In this connection, symbolism and protocol are important, and this means recognizing the importance of religious figures: receiving local representatives in their official capacity, as for other religions, and no longer in what is often a paternalistic gesture of rewarding the "good" and isolating the "wicked." Neutrality toward dogma must operate in both directions; there should be neither an effort to have pleasant things said to secular imams nor a grant of authority to religious interlocutors over the segment of the population of Muslim origin that does not recognize itself in them, by giving them a monopoly over the representation of Muslims in general. The danger lies in dealing with immigration through Islam and the *banlieues* through the mosque. Instead of combating the religious phenomenon, which will make it into an identity marker for organizing protest, it should be treated as purely religious and not as a tool for social management, even negatively—that is, by making militant *laïcité* that tool (which amounts to consecrating the most fundamentalist of the religious as competitors, as representing an alternative).

In short, nothing should be done with regard to dogma, and representatives of a faith should be considered as religious figures who have only the spiritual authority freely granted to them by the voluntary members of a purely religious community. Yet this means dealing with the fundamentalists, because any a priori exclusion of them would contradict the declared goal. But the campaign in defense of *laïcité* that we are witnessing today is aimed precisely at defining the neofundamentalists and other revivalists as enemies. But the forms of fundamentalism that are now emerging are far from systematically representing a threat, and in any event they reflect an evolution that has to be dealt with if we want to remain within the framework of democracy and the respect for human rights.

Intégralisme, Communitarianism, and Secularism

I take the term *intégralisme* from an excellent, critical, but not polemical article by Dominique Avon on Tariq Ramadan that shows that these questions can be seriously debated.[10] *Intégralisme* is indeed a form of fundamentalism, but one that no longer concerns society as a whole, for society has been secularized, but the believer who is attempting to live completely (*intégralement*) his faith as an individual: he attempts to do this not within the confines of a sect or a ghetto but in a process of negotiation with the authorities and the dominant society. *Intégralisme* looks for compromises but not concessions, because dogma is never put in question. *Intégralisme* is the modern form of fundamentalism, in the sense that it has integrated the loss of the social prominence of the sacred and its individualization while not calling dogma into question. For the believer, *intégralisme* consists of sanctifying his everyday life and placing everything under the sign of religion.[11] Culture and society are no longer the bearers of religious sentiment, which is based on radical individual reform followed by the establishment of a voluntary community of believers.

This kind of *intégralisme* is a characteristic of neofundamentalism in all religions. It has an obviously communitarian aspect insofar as believers ask for total respect for their faith, subject to negotiated arrangements to respect public order and the presence of others. A very interesting case occurred in the province of Ontario that carried multiculturalist logic to the extreme (it is, in fact, neocommunitarian, since communities are defined by religion, not ethnic origin). The provincial legislature, in a 1991 law on arbitration, accepted the de facto establishment of community dispute-settlement tribunals (Orthodox Jewish and Muslim, but the list is obviously open-ended) that deal with conflicts and questions of personal status provided that provincial and federal laws are not infringed and the parties involved have agreed to submit their case to the community tribunal (for example, a couple seeking a divorce—it being understood that the real divorce can be pronounced by only an official court). Similarly, in Montreal in 2001, a court authorized the Hassidic community to establish an *eruv* in an apartment complex that included secular residents in order to demarcate a private religious space within a public one.[12] Unthinkable in France, requests of this kind, in this instance coming from Orthodox Jews, are made by believers of all stripes who claim the right, so to speak, to duplicate profane space with a sacred mark that, meaning nothing to nonbelievers, could not possibly offend or limit them (for example, some Muslims have asked that meat in school cafeterias all be *hallal*, arguing that it makes no difference for non-Muslims, whereas the difference is essential for believers). We can clearly see that in the case of Ontario, compared with France, it is a completely different conception of the state (based on common law and contract) that makes it possible to accept the idea of community courts: the state does not intervene in a social bond defined by consenting adults. Incidentally, these civil arbitration courts were modeled on commercial arbitration courts, which clearly demonstrates the predominance of civil society over state-centered law but also the importance of economic liberalism in the production of a vision of society.

Public opinion obviously often sees this kind of demand as exorbitant, and, even in a multicultural society like Canada, it meets strong resistance: while the establishment of a rabbinical court passed unnoticed in Ontario, the announcement by the lawyer Syed Mumtaz Ali of the setting up of a sharia court provoked a hue and cry directed not at the principle of the court but at the fact that sharia discriminated against women.

What we can thus see being reformulated is the very concept of Muslim community in the view of the neofundamentalists; it is closed, to be sure, but explicitly conceived as a minority community in de facto secularized surroundings: they recognize the secularization of the public square, but they want to take their place in it as religious beings. Rather than a conquest of society, this is a form of privatization of public space. In this sense, fundamentalism is not incompatible with secularism but raises a question as to its relationship to the state. The debate on apostasy points in the same direction. It should be noted that in Muslim countries where the question has arisen, eminent fundamentalists have not called for the death of apostates but for their legal exclusion from the category of "Muslims." In Egypt, for example, they called for the annulment of the marriage of the thinker Nasr Abu Zayd, on the pretext that, since he was no longer a Muslim because of his critical writings on religion, he could not be married to a Muslim woman. In Pakistan, the violent campaign conducted by Abul Ala Maududi against the Qadyanis (or Ahmediyya) in the 1950s was aimed at having them declared a non-Muslim minority (whereas, in contrast, a similar campaign against the Bahai in Iran was aimed at converting them back to Islam, because what was at stake in that country were reasons of state, seen, of course, from the viewpoint of the mullahs, for Bahaism almost triumphed in the nineteenth century and challenged the profoundly national character of Iranian Shiism). Behind the radical flavor of these campaigns there emerges a vision of Muslims forming a purely religious community from which one may exclude oneself (or be excluded). This is to accept de facto a secular space, one where the laws of religion do not apply.

The neofundamentalist enterprise, by defining the community of believers not in sociological and cultural terms but as a voluntary association, has de facto constructed a space "other" than that of the surrounding society, thereby separating the religious from the social. The rule applies to only the believer.

But this neocommunitarian conception, often shared by other religions, poses a problem for *laïcité*, because it presupposes the establishment of sanctified spaces in the public square. There are two juxtaposed spaces that are no longer separated: the believer lives his religion in a space shared with the nonbeliever, but he inhabits that space in a different way. *Laïcité à la française* cannot accept that, because it is the state that defines public space, which cannot possibly be polysemous. And this is the source of the current tensions. Simply, this religious occupation of space should not be read as a forerunner of the seizure of political power. It is tied to the mutation of the religious realm in general and not to the extension of Islam, even if its visibility owes a good deal to the demographic weight of Muslims in the West.

The point is that neofundamentalism and its *intégraliste* view of religion are only one possible element in the range of choices available. There are many other forms that are less visible precisely because they are not controversial.

From Norm to Value

Once again, the problem is not dogma but religiosity. Liberal Muslims who accept the idea of a reformation of Islam or the tinkerers who are content to live their religion as they can in parallel with their social integration pose no problem for *laïcité* and are thus outside the purview of this study.

We should guard against identifying religious reform as a condition for the acceptance of *laïcité*. Many very conservative Muslims have adapted very well to secularization and to *laïcité* by reformulating their faith in terms of values rather than norms, along the lines followed by Christian conservatives.[13] They defend the family, sexual difference, and the criticism of morals; they oppose homosexual marriage and even abortion and divorce (two categories that hardly cause any difficulties in traditional sharia); but they remain within the framework of legality: this is exactly, once again, the position of Rocco Buttiglione, the unfortunate European commissioner, whose positions are, in the end, close to those of Tariq Ramadan (both condemn sexual freedom as contrary to the sacredness of life but reject coercive measures). Centrist but conservative Islam is being restructured following the Catholic, even the Orthodox Jewish, model (for example, on the issue of dietary prohibitions). Of course, we may wonder how all these fundamentalists would have behaved if they had found themselves on the Iberian Peninsula between the tenth and sixteenth centuries, far from the myth of the tolerant and multireligious Andalusia. But the question is abstract, because it is existing political systems that establish the scope of activity for each individual. This movement from legal norm to value is what makes acceptance of the rules of the game possible, which is the basis for *laïcité* and democracy. It is taken for granted by traditionalist Muslims living in the West, but obviously much less so by the born again and the converts.

The debate is therefore really a debate about values; however, we are not dealing with two opposed value systems of East and West but rather with a debate internal to the West bearing on the definition of the family (abortion, homosexuality, the position of women, artificial reproduction)—that is, the definition of the relationship between nature and freedom. Integrated Muslims have therefore increasingly reformulated their beliefs according to the terms of the Western debate.

Finally, other Muslims express themselves in the register of mysticism, pietism, or social action (sermons against drugs and violence). All registers are possible, but these integrated or silent forms pose no problem either for *laïcité* or for secularization. They are therefore simply forgotten in the debate, whereas they prove in actual fact the compatibility of Islam, *laïcité*, and secularism.

The Fantasy of Communitarianism

Laïcité is seen as a weapon to combat what is called communitarianism, defined at two levels: the neighborhood and the supranational *umma*—that is, the two levels at which society feels itself to be in crisis. But these two forms of communitarianism are in fact largely virtual and in any case unconnected in reality. The local community imagines itself in relation to the large virtual community of the *umma*, which exists only in the imagination or on the Internet. The idea that communitarianism might unify all the Muslims of any particular country makes no sense. We can clearly see in France that communitarianism is always established below (*banlieues*) or beyond society (the virtual *umma*), never at the level of society itself: there is no Muslim community in France but a scattered, heterogeneous population not very concerned with unifying itself or even with being really represented (evident in the poverty of cultural life; the weakness of voluntary organizations; the lack of Muslim religious schools; indifference to the Conseil français du culte musulman, which is kept going by the state but is not challenged in any way by any other, popular organization; the absence of political mobilization for elections or demonstrations). The Muslim community has even less substance than the Jewish community in France; there are rather very diversified populations, only one segment of which agrees to recognize itself as primarily a religious community.

Communitarianization is not spontaneous: it is the creation of communitarian leaders who claim to speak in the name of all in order to have themselves recognized by the state, which is in search of interlocutors and, in return, backs its interlocutors' status as representatives of a community (the president of the republic and government ministers systematically speak of the Jewish or Muslim community). The state rejects communitarianization while it has this word "community" constantly on its lips. Institutional communitarianization is an effect of a demand by the state, whereas, in the neighborhoods, it is the consequence of the reestablishment of broken social ties. In any event, if a Muslim community really existed, it would not have taken the government fifteen years to create a representative body for the Muslims of France, which would disintegrate in one day without the state's backing.

But what does communitarianization mean in local neighborhoods? What is the relationship among the social, ethnic, and religious components? In this area, we lack statistical tools. It is probable that the so-called difficult neighborhoods contain a concentration of immigrants and their descendants higher than was the case in the 1970s and 1980s. It is certain that two phenomena are occurring there in parallel: the establishment of a new form of social control through supervision by others (neighbors, adolescents), which concentrates primarily on girls; and the installation of mosques, some of which are more radical than others. But we are witnessing developments that are far from being homogeneous and leading to the establishment of ghettoized religious communities. The projects (*les cités*) are caught between the atomization of social relations and attempts to reconstruct social bonds. These attempts may take different forms, but obviously whoever says "social bond" means at the same time restoration of social control; only the models are variable: association of people coming from the same regions, the observance of Ramadan (also by non-Muslims) more as a festive than as a religious expression, the role of groups of young men in the occupation of space and the control of the few cultural organizations. The macho aspect of the young men of the *banlieues* has been thoroughly described, and the movement Ni putes ni soumises (Neither Whores nor Submissive) was established in defense of the young women of such areas. The community in this instance is seen as the closing of a territory on the basis of religious criteria around a population of foreign origin that has willingly broken with the republic. The fantasy, in fact, goes very far. For instance, the murder of a young woman named Ghofrane by blows from a rock in a Marseille immigrant neighborhood on October 18, 2004, was immediately called a stoning when it was really a crime of passion.[14] In the "RER D" affair, a young woman claimed she was taken for a Jew, a black man painted a swastika on her stomach, and a group of *beurs* threw her baby on the station platform. Although completely improbable (even if violence and anti-Semitism exist in the *banlieues*), the story was taken seriously by people who see the *banlieues* only in abstract reconstructions like the ones Pierre-André Taguieff sets out, where Islamism has become a version of Nazism. Since the young men of the *banlieues* are described as little Nazis, we expect to see them act like little Nazis. What is developing is a new image of the dangerous classes, like the one that arose in the nineteenth century.

But what these analyses fail to see is the heterogeneity of immigrant neighborhoods, the quite relative character of their isolation, and also the variable strength of religious control. The proliferation of mosques is as much the sign of a fragmentation of Muslims as an affirmation of their identity. The mosques are, in fact, more often than not rivals: on top of the old ethnic divisions (that still exist) among Moroccans, Algerians, Turks, and so on, have now been piled ideological oppositions (Salafi mosque against traditional mosque), generational conflicts (young men who no longer want the imam "from the old country"), and conflicts between groups (the Tabligh mosque, the Ahbash mosque, and so on). In addition, social control is quite relative and does not at all prevent deviant behavior. Macho attitudes are just as prevalent among the young black and Latino men of American inner cities, and they have nothing Muslim about them. Finally, far from being sequestered, young women generally know how to manage their relationships, but outside the space of the neighborhood. One leaves the neighborhood, in fact, precisely when one no longer corresponds to the prevalent stereotypes (in a mixed marriage, for example, particularly when a Muslim girl marries a non-Muslim) but also because of social mobility (acquiring property), which has the paradoxical effect of reinforcing the reputation of the immigrant neighborhood for poverty and social exclusion. The focus on the neighborhoods means that the emergence of a Muslim middle class has not been noticed by politicians. Finally, as is often the case in studies concerning women, they are made into a distinct group, dominated under constraint or reproducing that constraint through the internalization of the norms that justify it: trapped between domination and alienation, women can be liberated only through the law. These analyses forget that most girls who want to wear the veil in school demand it in the name of their freedom and their personal choice and often as a means of asserting themselves without breaking ties with their social milieu. Although violence certainly exists, strategies are varied, and neighborhood identity is often shared by its inhabitants regardless of sex.[15]

Because the bulk of the problems of the *banlieues* is attributed to Islam, authoritarian *laïcité* has been designated as a tool to deal with these problems while ignoring (or devaluing) other elements. Not only has this policy failed to meet its goals (because the Muslim woman has not been waiting in pained silence for the law to liberate her, especially if she is a single mother, clandestine, or on welfare), but it has had the opposite effect. In thereby making *laïcité* a repressive device, we have helped both to put religion at the heart of the debate and to present it as an alternative. As a consequence, Islam is set up as the dominant marker among the children of immigrants (consider the terminological slippage of Minister of the Interior Nicolas Sarkozy when he appointed a descendant of immigrants as a prefect, calling him a "Muslim prefect"). The identification between Arab and Muslim is strengthened by leaving aside secular Muslims, to be sure violently opposed to Salafism but finding it difficult to bring forth another identity (see, for example, the Mouvement des maghrébins laïques de France [Movement of Secular North Africans of France]). Because Islam has been made into the prism through which the question of immigration is seen, especially the problems of integration, we are brought, for lack of a global policy, to make intervention in the religious sphere a prerequisite. Rather than a reminder of *laïcité*, this is a distortion of its very principles.

The term "Islam" is used today to give unity to a complex assemblage of conduct, demands, and identities that really become meaningful only when they are considered laterally, either in relation to other similar attitudes without religious reference points or, on the contrary, in relation to similar behavior in other religions. Islam is thus turned into an essence, as though it has become the invariant that determines attitudes in very different contexts. A murder with blows from a rock is defined as a stoning. The macho attitudes of young men in the *banlieues*, regrettably similar in very different contexts (from Los Angeles to Moscow), is attributed to Islam. Adolescents' intentions to assert themselves by wearing provocative clothing is a banality in secondary schools, but the affair of the veil has been experienced as the penetration of the school system by Islamism. A girl wearing the veil wants simultaneously to assert herself as an individual, escape from the social constraint of her milieu by adopting a sign that grants her both value and autonomy, make herself noticed, affirm a form of authenticity, and on and on. There is very clearly an "Islam of the young," made up of a complex mixture of generational conflict, a search for authenticity going beyond the parents' generation, and an affirmation of identity *and* protest.[16] I am not talking about being indulgent, and young people should, in fact, be challenged about the collective meaning of their individual attitudes, about their social responsibility, and about the connotations of what for some of them is a mere banality (anti-Semitic insults). But a systematic attack against Islam can only strengthen them in their identification of revolt, protest, and adolescent crisis with religion. These generational phenomena are by definition transitional, but they are also attributed to an immutable culture, thereby transforming the young person into the object of a manipulation, whereas he wants, on the contrary, to assert himself as a subject.

Many young people of Muslim background have therefore developed complex strategies by themselves, manipulating the reference to Islam. They have exploited Islam as much as their detractors. A typical case, which I have already mentioned, is that of girls: by defining them essentially as victims, we leave them no choice for their emancipation but a break with their family circle, whereas very few of them wish for that (and, besides, some of the social problems of the *banlieues* stem more from the disintegration of families than from the burden of family structures). The debate on marriage is a sign of this misunderstanding: the press speaks constantly of the number of forced marriages, most of which are not forced but arranged; that is, the girl agrees to play along, while later possibly escaping with profit or at least with honor intact. For example, she will marry a cousin from the old country, which grants him a residence permit, and later divorce him with honor intact. Such complex relations, to be sure, frequently lead to tragedy, but to turn them into a mechanism for enslavement amounts to positing freedom in abstraction, paying no attention to emotional ties, even if they are conflicted, between parents and children, or to the wish of children to take their place in a given family genealogy. The discourse of women's liberation here comes up against the reality experienced by these young women, which is far from being one of systematic enslavement. We often experience with reference to North African girls a liberation by proxy, a continuation of the battles of the 1960s. In fact, abstractions about Islam, the youth of the *banlieues*, and the North African woman mask much more complex and contradictory human realities. Improvised expressions of quests for identity are systematically over-Islamized, relegating social actors to an essentialist identity, whereas they are engaged in a dynamic search for themselves.

This same essentialist reading is applied to political violence. There is no doubt that Bin Laden calls for jihad, but the violence he puts into operation (and that he stages) and the attraction he holds for many young men also operates in other registers, particularly that of a quite European extreme leftist anti-imperialism. Every reference to the Koran by Bin Laden, Zawahiri, or Zarqawi is dissected, but as far as I know no one has pointed out that the macabre staging of hostage executions in Iraq (a tribunal, today Islamic, in the past revolutionary, standing behind the victim, beneath a banner bearing the name and logo of the organization, prisoner confessions, the reading of the sentence by a masked man, and so on) is borrowed directly from the extreme Left of the 1970s, in particular from the staging of the "trial" of Aldo Moro by the Italian Red Brigades in 1978.

We thus have a twofold exploitation of the reference to Islam: by Muslim actors (youth in a protest posture or people with the ambition of becoming community leaders) and by those who think that Islam is a problem. All of them systematically emphasize the reference to Islam.

But scraping away the labels, putting in perspective the behavior attributed to Islam both in time (the generational crisis) and in social space (other religions), we can see that the strictly religious content is reduced. The revival of religion is occurring in a secularized world; it is even an emblem of it, because it bears secularization within itself.

4

DE FACTO SECULARIZATION

Muslims today find themselves in a position rather comparable to that of Catholics in the nineteenth century: they have come to terms with *laïcité* through political steps, not through theological reformation, as can be seen, for example, with the establishment of the Conseil français du culte musulman. As for the Catholic Church, the question of institutional organization has preceded the debate on theology. The acceptance of secular authority by religious leaders and the recognition of the autonomy of religion by state authorities are indeed political decisions. The degree of sincerity or calculation involved is of little importance: it is the political realm that defines the respective positions of religion and politics and not the converse, from Islamic Iran to France.

Politics creates *laïcité*: this is also true insofar as the West provides broader intellectual freedom for Muslim thinkers along with both less state control and more stimulation. There is no reason to believe that state censorship comes primarily from clerical states like Iran. Authoritarian secular states are often just as hostile to theological innovation as they are to fundamentalism. They almost always favor conservative Islam, as we saw in the Algeria of the Front de libération nationale, because they are suspicious of any form of intellectual freedom and critique, even in the restricted realm of theology. What is positive in the West is its religious indifference, not its willed attempts to control religion.

But, as for Catholicism, political acceptance of *laïcité* is possible only because a process of secularization has taken place, either acknowledged or disregarded by the participants. For liberated, moderate, or secular Muslims, this ambient secularism is experienced in a positive way. But it is also operative in fundamentalism, through the two major vectors of religious renewal: the individualization of religiosity and the loss of cultural identity, which has prevented the emergence of a natural community of believers and condemned all communitarianization to being only voluntary and hence the realm of a minority. This is why the question of the sincerity of fundamentalists who say they respect *laïcité* does not need to be asked, because they have no choice: the means that have led to their success presuppose precisely that secularization has been accomplished.

The assertion of a Muslim religious identity in the West assumes a change in the cultural and social anchoring of religion—that is, the establishment of a religious space different from what it was in more traditional societies. This implies a gap between real practices and representations, which obliges the individual to redefine his personal relationship to religion and to adapt practices that no longer have the same meaning in different contexts. Hence the practice of Islam as a minority religion requires thinking through secularization and *laïcité* rather than experiencing them passively in an illusion of social conformity. It is indeed the concrete practice of Muslims and not a new theology that has shaped a new relationship to secularization and *laïcité*. One of these concrete practices is indeed political action, which is not confined to the desire to establish an Islamic state. The failure of political Islam—that is, the impossibility (whatever the reasons) of establishing an Islamic state instituting peace, social justice, development, and reconciliation between religious utopia and modernity—has, in fact, been confirmed by most Islamic figures.[1] Although many of them have been converted to support for parliamentary government (like the Adalet ve Kalkinma [AK; Justice and Development] Party in Turkey), there was no need for them to have become ideological liberals and democrats (no more than Monsignor Lavigerie was a Christian Democrat before the fact: he was a monarchist before the toast of Algiers, and he remained one afterward). Among new practices has been the experience of Islam as a minority religion, which is true for immigrants and their descendants, but also for Turkish Islamists, who very quickly had to give up their hope of securing a monopoly of political representation for Islam in a country where more than 80 percent of the population define themselves as believing Muslims (observance is something else). The municipal Islamism tried out by the young leaders of the Turkish Refah (Welfare) Party (among whom was Tayyip Erdoğan, elected mayor of Istanbul in 1994) led them toward a pluralist political practice, somewhat in the way that municipal Communism in France in the middle of the twentieth century detached many mayors belonging to the French Communist Party from Stalinism. It is, in fact, participation in the political process that leads believers with little inclination toward democracy as a social ideal to accept the rules of the game and often to become strong defenders of those rules. If we had to wait for everyone to become a democrat before creating democracy, France would still be a monarchy. Institutions have a very great capacity for integration provided they make no ideological demands (in France, we guarded against making such demands on Catholics as well as Communists). It can, of course, always be argued that the acceptance of democracy by the Communists and by the Catholic Church was a matter of power relations: the church had everything to lose from a struggle for power, and the strategic balance between the Soviet Union and NATO barred the French and Italian Communist Parties from any possibility of a coup de force. But the same argument holds for Islam: on the strategic and military level, the Muslim world (which has never existed as a bloc) is beaten, crushed, and dominated and is even incapable of using the oil weapon. In fact, the "Muslim world" is not a geostrategic concept, because it has never had a concrete political or military embodiment (the Ottoman Empire was indeed a geostrategic entity, but it was Ottoman before it was Muslim, as China has always been Chinese before being Communist). Although the current strategic context may lead young men to choose to identify themselves with an imaginary community and join the jihad, it is having the deeper and more long-range result of leading Muslims, moderates and neofundamentalists alike, to rethink the way in which they are integrated into Western societies, by recognizing that the radicals have distorted the political imaginative structures they hold in common.

Islam has thus been transformed, on the one hand, by a process of the secularization of society (one of whose manifestations is paradoxically the ambient re-Islamization, because you re-Islamize what has been secularized) and, on the other, by a negotiated political integration, as illustrated by the establishment of the Conseil français du culte musulman. Hence, in every Western country, Islam is being integrated not following its own traditions but according to the place that each society has defined for religion, from Anglo-Saxon indulgence to Gallic suspicion, although the former needs to be less naive and the latter less pathological.

Politics Creates *Laïcité*:
The Case of the Union des organisations islamiques de France

The question often arises as to how, then, to reconcile *laïcité* with the fundamentalist positions of the Union des organisations islamiques de France. But it is not the content of the UOIF's positions that count. As I have said, we do not ask Monsignor Lustiger to declare from the pulpit that abortion is not a crime but that he not incite fundamentalists to attack abortion clinics; in short, we ask him to respect the law and public order, not to adapt his beliefs to the law. This is exactly the same demand that should be addressed to Muslim organizations. Yet they are constantly questioned about sharia. What the state asks of them is what it asks of every citizen: not to incite murder and even less to commit one, under threat of the penalties provided by law. In fact, the state does not have to adapt to Islam: it suffices that it maintain the secular line, understood as a legal tool, not an ideology (which it has tended to become).

And this distinction between the law of the state and the law of God has already been incorporated by the UOIF and by figures such as Tariq Ramadan. When Ramadan proposes a moratorium on the punishments provided by sharia, he is at bottom more secular than the government minister who asks him to declare the veil optional, because he recognizes the distinction between the two orders: public political space and religious space. The moratorium affects the public space without touching dogma. Ramadan, like any other Islamic leader, is required to explain himself only with regard to public space.

We wonder about the sincerity of those involved. This is a naive approach, because the people in question have adopted a political stance (in the strong sense of the word), and politics has little to do with sincerity: when Monsignor Lavigerie called for recognition of the republic, he nonetheless probably remained a sincere monarchist, but he acted in a situation in which the fact of the republic seemed to him unavoidable (we should not forget that the same Lavigerie who recognized the republic founded the order of White Fathers with the goal of converting Muslims—with the approval of that republic). The fact of the secular state is inescapable today, in France as in Turkey, because it has been incorporated by society. Suspicion is kept up by the fact that the UOIF, like Ramadan, belongs, at least by intellectual ancestry, to the current of the Muslim Brotherhood.

But the two aspects that are problematic in the UOIF and Ramadan (Salafism and political Islamism) are precisely means for political integration. Salafism shatters the cultural reference to the Middle East and makes it possible to define a pure religion, detached from its ethnic elements, and hence to adapt it to a loss of cultural identity otherwise experienced as traumatic. By insisting on the individualization of the approach, acting primarily on the young, and promoting a return to Islam, in a way often close to born-again Protestants, Salafists of every kind have helped to break up imported communities to the benefit of another community, that of the believers who have decided to recognize themselves in it. But this is the definition of any church, any community of saints. The question then becomes that of the relationship between a religious community and the state.

And it is here that the second aspect of the UOIF plays a role: its Muslim Brotherhood ancestry. For members of the Brotherhood have always been politicians, what I call Islamists. They dreamed of an Islamic state, but they were transformed by their political practice after confronting states and experiencing social and political constraints (the fact of the nation, for example). It was a failure, and not only because of repression. In more than sixty years of political practice, the Islamists have evolved, like many former Marxist revolutionaries. Today they lead a moderate and pro-European government in Turkey (which rejects, a little hypocritically, any allusion to its Islamist past). In France, their innovation in politics has come from their reflection on the concept of minority. Islam is in the minority. Religious identity is constructed without reference to the state, and the law will never be anything but the law that the believer is willing to adopt. From there, only two directions are possible: toward a sect that places itself on the fringes of a society that it will never control (these are the most fundamentalist groups, but they can be entirely quietist) or else toward a representative organization that demands recognition for the citizen-believer.

The community is a construction that makes sense only if people voluntarily join it. And the creation of voluntary communities had nothing antirepublican about it, even if an old individualistic egalitarianism hovered over the baptismal font of our republic (we recall the Le Chapelier law passed during the Revolution banning all coalitions, including unions). But the Rousseauist myth of a republic where there is nothing between the state and the citizen-individual in his isolation (the "silence of the passions," for passion is always the other) has long been nothing but a legal and philosophical fiction—to be sure, a founding fiction, but one that means nothing in political sociology.

What does the UOIF want? Recognition of the Muslim citizen. That is, of a citizen who sees himself as Muslim above all but who accepts and recognizes the laws of the republic. Concretely, since the veil is a religious obligation, the UOIF cannot say that it is optional (the UOIF is joined here by the rector of the Paris Mosque, Dalil Boubakeur), but if the veil is banned in school, then the UOIF reserves its right to take legal action in an effort to change the law. The crisis created by the seizure of two French reporters as hostages in Iraq in September 2004 enabled various Islamic organizations in France to put this distinction into practice: the hostage takers demanded the abrogation of the law banning the wearing of the veil in school; the Muslims of France massively rejected this outside intervention and expressed their solidarity with the position of the French government. What more could be asked for? The different spaces are clearly distinguished: the law is a French matter that can and must be challenged within the legal framework of the republic. One may thus disapprove of a law while asserting one's citizenship: there is no contradiction in that in a democratic state. This is very precisely what one can expect from a religious organization that respects *laïcité*. It does not compromise its values, but it recognizes the law—that is, the distinction between the two orders: public and political space, on the one hand, and religious space, on the other. *Laïcité* is nothing but that.

But there can obviously be no question of recognizing anyone as holding a monopoly on the representation of the Muslims of

France; the UOIF is only one actor among others. Room for plurality must be preserved.

Laïcité, Secularization, and Theology

There is no direct link, and even less a causal one, among the three levels: secularization of society, political *laïcité*, and religious reformism. But a deep disturbance of the sociological bases of religion cannot help being reflected at one point or another in religious thought, as we have seen in the case of Catholicism: the aggiornamento came after, not before, the acceptance of *laïcité*. This is what will happen for Islam. The shock for Islam has been the loss of the social prominence of religion—that is, its embodiment in a culture, and its reduction to a social and political minority, followed by its reconstruction as a pure religion, on an individual basis, even if that leads to the reconstruction of a territorially unattached community of believers.

This kind of upheaval in so short a period of time will necessarily have consequences, and they may be contradictory. The Catholic Church was traversed by very diverse and complex movements after it reluctantly accepted *laïcité* and secularization. That had consequences that were not only theological but also ecclesiastical (what is the meaning of the church as institution?). The same thing is true for Islam, but here the comparison must be made with Protestantism as well, because, by definition, there is no central authority capable of grasping hold of the process and channeling it by bestowing legitimacy on it (as Vatican II did for Catholicism) or even by censuring it (as with the Vatican's banning of worker-priests in 1953). Theological liberalization will probably be a consequence of the political acceptance of *laïcité* by Muslims, but the choice has already been made in practice by the mass of Muslims who have adapted without difficulty, whereas all attention is concentrated on those who pose problems. Theological aggiornamento is not a prerequisite for the emergence of a liberal Islam in practice but will probably be able to give it theological legitimacy after the fact.

The problem in fact lies in the definition of the market for religion: as we have seen, the second generation of French Muslims is not buying an intellectual and complex Islam for many reasons (the most important being that they want to experience immediately a total Islam that has the answers to everything). But the emergence of middle classes has changed things (along, no doubt, with the aging of militants and their settling down to family life) and created a demand for a more sophisticated religious formulation. Behind the label "Islam" there are men and women, Muslims of flesh and blood, with their social and economic expectations and their integration into a complex society, well beyond ghettos, *banlieues*, and housing projects. They need a more diversified offering, so to speak, of religious products, and it is this diversity that ought to be encouraged. But for that we will precisely have to avoid freezing polarized identities and hence avoid systematically politicizing religion.

Laïcité creates religion by making it a category apart that has to be isolated and circumscribed. It reinforces religious identities rather than allowing them to dissolve in more diversified practices and identities. In the incessant quest for any sign of communitarianization, in order to denounce it, the current campaign being conducted against Islam is helping precisely to reify Islam and turn it in on itself, whereas many of the forms of what has been defined as the revival of religion and of communitarianization are, rather, attempts to escape from that essentialist identity (which claims that Islam is a culture, a religion, and a community all at once). The forms of the return of Islam have to be considered laterally to see that they are also in their way an attempt to respond to the challenges of integration while preserving an identity, sometimes all the more virulent because it is purely formal.

But stigmatizing religion puts many moderate or even nonreligious Muslims in an awkward position; they have the same identity problems as many fundamentalists but have not come up with the same responses, which has led to contrasting attitudes: North African intellectuals fighting against the radical Islam in their countries may also be offended by the demonization of girls wearing the veil in French schools. The individual choice of many French Muslims is precisely not to put their religion forward. They spontaneously live it out in a secular fashion. But, obliged to justify themselves, aware also that the question is not simply about the beard and the veil but that other elements are in play (social structures, racism, integration, sentimental attachment to an Arab identity even though it is not expressed by any activism or any demand for recognition), they feel all the more ill at ease in the radical campaign for *laïcité* because they do not see the question as a battle between good and evil.

For, while there is a debate about values, that debate is an internal one for the West. The American election campaign and the refusal of the European Parliament to ratify the appointment of Rocco Buttiglione show that the question of values is dividing the West. Against the liberal and open tradition that we like to see as the sign of Europe, there is, in the same West, a conservative reaction that defends the family, wants to limit abortion, rejects same-sex marriage, and is troubled by what it sees as an excessive liberalization of morality. It is opposed to a West that champions the liberation movements of the 1960s, feminism, minority rights, democratization, homosexual rights, and the like. The entry of Islam into the debate has shifted the boundaries. At first accepted by the second group in the name of multiculturalism and the defense of the Third World and of immigrants (hence in a context characterized as minority), Islam was rejected by the first in the name of history (from the Crusades to the Reconquista to the Algerian War) and the Christian identity of Europe. But in the course of the 1990s, the Islamic referent shifted from one domain to the other. Now defending values more than a culture, conservative Muslims find themselves in the camp of the conservative Christians, and they use the same formulation: the defense of family values. But they have not been welcomed with open arms by those Christians, who are firmly focused on the defense of identity. At the same time, the shift from the oppressed immigrant to the demanding Muslim has alienated the progressive Left and made it possible to establish a bridge between that Left and the so-called modern populists (who take the sexual liberation of the 1960s for granted and do not recognize themselves in the old-guard language of the Right and the extreme Right).[2] This was typically the position of Pym Fortuyn and Theo Van Gogh in Holland.

This migration of the Muslim reference from the defense of the immigrant (and of multiculturalism) to a defense of conservative values has deeply disturbed the patterns according to which political and moral positions are adopted in Europe. But in all this internal migration in the realm of European representations, Islam has merely aligned itself with Western sets of problems and contributed neither an alternative nor a challenge to what a European identity might be. The example of the coming to power of the former Islamists of the AK Party in Turkey is interesting: in the summer of 2004, the government tried to get a law passed prohibiting adultery. This could be seen as a surreptitious attempt to Islamize a perfectly secular legal system. In fact, however, this law had nothing to do with sharia, because it defined the married couple according to the Western model (a monogamous couple in which the partners are equal); it was more a copy of the revival of religious values, as in the United States (where ten states have and apply a similar law) than a means of getting closer to Saudi Arabia. Believers in Turkey are closer to Christian religious conservatives than to Arab Islamists. We may be worried by the fact, but to every man his Europe. For, more than ever, it is the West that determines the debate about values, a debate within which an Islam detached from any particular culture is being reformulated.

Islam has thus indeed been transformed by both secularization and *laïcité*. Liberals, moderates, freethinkers, and simple pragmatists have long resolved the question of how to live their faith (or its absence) in Western society. Today's fundamentalism in all its forms is an attempt to respond to that challenge by putting a religious identity in the forefront. It has developed as a discourse, and it is attempting to re-create a space, a territory, in which the individual can completely live his faith. But this space is virtual, between the myth of an *umma* that can be encountered only on the Internet and a local community, closed in on itself, that survives only because the outside world appears to it to be hostile. It is indeed Islam that is now confronting the challenge of *laïcité* and secularism, and the arrogance of a few young neophytes who think that the Western world, bogged down in its materialism, can only massively join the camp of the true believers should not make us forget that that Islam has bowed to the new configurations, from territorial detachment to individualization, not so much because of theological reform as because it has now learned to live as a minority. What I have attempted to show here is that even fundamentalism has at bottom incorporated the religious space of the West (individualism, separation between politics and religion) and is striving to promote its conservative, indeed reactionary, values in a discourse and practice that mirror those of Christian and Jewish conservatives. The problem is not Islam but religion or, rather, the contemporary forms of the revival of religion. This is not a reason to show indulgence in solidarity with those who seem to be excluded but rather an invitation to think about Islam in the same framework as we think about other religions and about the religious phenomenon itself. This is true respect for the other and the true critical spirit.

NOTES

Preface

1. Olivier Roy, *Globalized Islam: The Search for a New Ummah* (New York: Columbia University Press, 2004).

2. This is the central theme of *Globalized Islam*.

3. Sharon Bernstein, "Making Shabbat a Day at the Beach: Venice-Area Jews Seek an Eruv to Ease Limits on Activities," *Los Angeles Times*, October 25, 2006.

4. Two recent books shed some light on the specificity of the French treatment of Muslims: Jonathan Laurence and Justin Vaisse, *Integration Islam: Political and Religious Challenges in Contemporary France* (Washington, D.C.: Brookings Institution Press, 2006); and John R. Bowen, *Why the French Don't Like Headscarves: Islam, the State, and Public Space* (Princeton, N.J.: Princeton University Press, 2006).

Introduction

1. For example, during the press campaign against Tariq Ramadan that caused a stir in 2004, a substantial number of articles mentioned

the fact that he was "handsome." What did that have to do with an intellectual discussion? The underlying (and very Christian) idea was a reference to the beauty of the devil—that is, an appearance designed to seduce. Ramadan, we were told, used words with dual meanings, and we were taken in, because he charmed both secular intellectuals and the young men of the *banlieues*. Fortunately, courageous investigators were there to guard and punish, like Caroline Fourest, author of the book *Frère Tariq*, who wrote: "We will have to assess the complicity of everyone who fostered the ascendancy of preachers like him" (*L'Express*, October 18, 2004). But what Ramadan has to say lies, in fact, in the realm of ideas and should be considered in that light. In my view, what was taken as the use of language with dual meanings arises from a contradiction in Ramadan's thinking, a contradiction that gives it all its interest, as this book will show. But since when is intellectual contradiction punishable as an instance of bad faith? The defenders of *laïcité* still display traces of the Catholic Inquisition.

2. To note two examples, books by Chahdortt Djavann, *Que pense Allah de l'Europe?* (Paris: Gallimard, 2004), and Christophe Deloire, *Les Islamistes sont déjà là* (Paris: Albin Michel, 2004), were on the best-seller lists in the fall of 2004, outselling all other books on Islam. The idea that critical discourse against Islam is a minority phenomenon struggling against the politically correct is obviously false: the book by Oriana Fallaci, claiming to speak in the name of a beleaguered minority, had a print run of more than a million copies in Italy. Newspaper articles and television talk shows frequently adopted a bellicose tone (like the article "Enquête sur les ennemis de la République," *L'Express*, January 26, 2004, and the report "Qui est vraiment Tariq Ramadan?" broadcast on *Envoyé spécial* on France 2, December 2, 2004).

3. Vincent Geisser, *La Nouvelle Islamophobie* (Paris: La Découverte, 2003); Xavier Ternisien, "Du racisme anti-arabe à l'islamophobie," *Le Monde*, October 10, 2003.

4. The banlieues are working-class suburbs, notably in the Paris region, now frequently inhabited by immigrants from North Africa and their descendants.—Trans.

5. Like the newspaper *La Croix*, in those far-off times. There were, however, also anticlerical anti-Semites, a tradition that survives with Jocelyn Bézecourt, for example, a member of the Union des familles laïques (Union of Secular Families), who writes for the Web site www.atheisme.org.

6. The local representative of the federation of parents' associations of students in the public schools (Cornec) of a lycée in Dreux in March 2004 distributed a leaflet referring to "groups of boys chasing unveiled girls in the streets of the town" and "graffiti in apartment buildings: 'Dreux for the Muslims'" (this was precisely one of the themes of the Front National campaigns in Dreux in the 1980s). The departmental federation reacted by dissolving the local section, and the local branch of a national antidiscrimination organization denounced the leaflet.

7. The case of Michèle Tribalat is an interesting one. In 1996, this demographer published a book, *De l'immigration à l'assimilation*, that was amazingly optimistic: everything was going well, and the immigrants would *Faire France* (the title of another of her books). Four years later (the blink of an eye for a demographer), she wrote *Dreux, voyage au cœur du malaise français*, a work that was just as excessive but in the other direction: all of a sudden, everything was going badly, communities no longer socialized, and there were no more mixed marriages (an observation that seems quite subjective for someone like me, an inhabitant of the town). What happened between 1996 and 2000? What event unknown to the general public (and many specialists) had tilted France toward a divorce from its immigrants? Either Tribalat had failed to see what was coming and her current assessment should be judged in light of her past amateurism, or else her view of the world has changed. But we ought to be told which it is.

8. There are 30,000 students in private Jewish schools ("Un tableau de l'école juive in France," *L'Arche*, no. 555 [May 2004]). In contrast, there are only a few dozen students in Muslim schools. The argument according to which Muslims are too poor to finance private schools, especially not under government contract, does not withstand scrutiny: it would probably be easy to find sponsors in the Persian Gulf states to finance Muslim schools of the kind. However, the nature of communitarian ties plays a

decisive role, which demonstrates by contrast that there is no Muslim community, for there is no solidarity among French Muslims in social and cultural activity. The case of the Conseil français du culte musulman (French Council of the Muslim Faith), held at arm's length by the Ministry of the Interior (and of Religious Organizations!), is also a good example of the resistance of those involved to their own communitarianization.

9. *Beurs* is slang term, formed by phonetic reversal of *Arabe*, for people born in France of North African immigrant parents; it is not a racist term.—Trans.

10. The journal *Cités*, edited by Yves-Charles Zarka, published on the cover of a special issue ("L'Islam en France," 2004) a cartoon in which a Muslim turns his back on the republic, a cover that is interesting in its ambiguity: judging by his dress and his physical appearance, the fundamentalist is clearly an Arab from the Middle East, but, keeping the outline of the drawing, if you were to replace the skullcap with a kippa and the Koran with the Torah, you would reproduce an anti-Semitic cartoon of the 1930s: a person with a hooked nose, badly shaved, swarthy, carrying the holy book, and turning his back on a blond and curvaceous Marianne brandishing the constitution.

11. Max Weber states it clearly: "A 'spirit' [*Geist*] is not confined to the religious formation that brings it into existence" (*Sociologie des religions* [Paris: Gallimard, 1996], 151).

1. French *Laïcité* and Islam

1. Marcel Gauchet, *La Religion dans la démocratie: Parcours de la laïcité* (Paris: Gallimard, 1998), particularly chap. 2, "Le Lieu et le moment," where *laïcité* is attributed to countries of Catholic tradition and secularization to Protestant Europe.

2. When approaching the question of Islam, most non-Muslim writers prefer to make a choice (the Islam of this or that) rather than to admit the diversity of responses that Muslim thought has contributed over time and in various places.

3. Jean Baubérot, *Laïcité (1905–2005) entre passion et raison* (Paris: Seuil, 2004); Henri Peña-Ruiz, *Qu'est-ce que la laïcité?* (Paris: Gallimard, 2003).

4. "*Laïcité* seems more than ever to be a comprehensive social program" (*L'Enseignement public*, no. 3 [November–December 1981]). The common program of the Left, drafted in 1972, which served as the platform for the election of François Mitterrand in 1981, declares: "True *laïcité*, based on the scientific spirit and democracy, provides a complete critical knowledge of reality and encompasses all aspects of life and human activity." These quotations are taken from an excellent article by Pierre Ognier, "Ancienne ou nouvelle laïcité? Après dix ans de débats," *Esprit*, August–September 1993. It is provocative to note that the last sentence, defining *laïcité* as a veritable ideology, echoes the Islamist thinker Ali Maududi, who defines Islam as "an all-encompassing concept dealing with life as an integrated whole." See Olivier Roy, *The Failure of Political Islam*, trans. Carol Volk (Cambridge, Mass.: Harvard University Press, 1994).

5. Peña-Ruiz, *Qu'est-ce que la laïcité?*; Didier Motchane, "L'Islam de France sera-t-il républicain?" *Confluences Méditerranée*, no. 32 (Winter 1999–2000). The title of the latter is interesting because it posits, first, the existence, desirable rather than observed, of an "Islam of France" (and not "in France") and, second, the necessity of a "republican" Islam (who would speak today of a "republican Catholicism"?). The underlying vision is thus that Islam in itself cannot possibly be republican and that France can and must transform its Islam. This vision, as I shall show, is more Gallican than secular. In an interview with the journal *Islam de France*, Motchane declared:

> Strictly speaking, *laïcité* is the implementation of the demand for equality in the world of the mind; in other words, it is the product of the exercise of "natural reason" in the realm of convictions. This requirement is probably not defined as such in this way anywhere but in Europe. It should not be reduced to the demand for the religious neutrality of the state and the recognition of freedom of conscience. It implies an unequivocal separation of public space from all private spaces.

But two lines later, he seriously qualifies his position:

On the other hand, *laïcité* itself, and in particular the provisions of the 1905 law, in no way deprive the state of the possibility of contributing to the creation of conditions that will give Muslims the feeling that they are living their culture and practicing their religion in the same way as the rest of the French population. We know, for example, that state and regional authorities can guarantee loans to finance the construction of religious buildings, for which municipalities can provide land under a long-term lease. (interview by Saïd Branine, "Les Difficultés d'une institution de l'Islam en France doivent être surmontées progressivement," *Islam de France*, October 1999, posted on www.oumma.com, on May 26, 2000)

6. Ognier, "Ancienne ou nouvelle laïcité?" 218.

7. A complex and excellent study of the philosophical approaches that can establish a basis for *laïcité* as a philosophical theory can be found in Guy Haarscher, *La Laïcité* (Paris: Presses Universitaires de France, 1996), chap. 4. But, once again, the political and legal definition of *laïcité* preceded any philosophical approach.

8. For a discussion of *laïcité* as a legal principle, see the voluminous and excellent Francis Messner, Pierre-Henri Prélot, and Jean-Marie Woehrling, eds., *Traité du droit français des religions* (*TDFR*) (Paris: Litec, Éditions du Juris-classeur, 2003), 393.

9. For example, in the case of a divorce litigated in France of a couple married in a foreign country under religious law, the court rejects religious authority not in the name of the principle of *laïcité* but in the name of the territoriality of the French legal system (*TDFR*, 653).

10. As he was getting ready to put through the separation laws, the high priest of militant *laïcité*, Émile Combes, followed a very conservative right-wing economic policy.

11. Circular of November 17, 1883, to elementary-school teachers: "Ask yourself if a father, I mean a single one, listening to you in your classroom, could in good faith refuse his assent to what you are about to say."

12. This position is very well epitomized by Pierre-André Taguieff:

The response of republicans, by definition defenders of the principle of *laïcité*, is to modernize Islam. This means first, in Muslim culture which tends to confuse them, distinguishing and separating the political and the religious. This amounts to fostering the appearance of a "secular Islam," compatible with the principles of pluralist democracy and the values of individualism (the privatization of faith). But if this "Islam *à la française*" is surely desirable, its emergence is blocked by a sizable sociopolitical obstacle: the weakening, not to say the crumbling, of nation-states in a period of globalization. To bring about the emergence of an "integrated" Islam, we have to rely on an integrating political structure, the founding principles of which are strongly adhered to by citizens and are capable of attracting candidates for integration. Is the French nation in its current state sufficiently attractive? Does France still possess enough influence to be able to compensate with national symbolic goods for the loss of some of the psychic nourishment provided by former systems of belief? ("Vous avez dit 'communautarisme'?" *Le Figaro*, July 17, 2003)

13. This is the meaning of article 35 of the 1905 law prohibiting the direct provocation by a minister of religion to resist the execution of laws. The interpretation according to which dogma may not be taken into account was recently confirmed by the Conseil d'État in a decision of June 2000 concerning two associations of Jehovah's Witnesses.

14. Nicolas Sarkozy, *La République, les religions, l'espérance* (Paris: Cerf, 2004).

15. Michèle Tribalat and Jeanne-Hélène Kaltenbach, *La République et l'Islam* (Paris: Gallimard, 2002), 162.

16. Tariq Ramadan, debate with Interior Minister Nicolas Sarkozy, November 20, 2003, on France 2. Ramadan refused to declare these laws null and void but called for a moratorium on them—that is, proposed that their application be abandoned, without abolishing them as such.

17. Baubérot, *Laïcité*, 93.

18. Motchane, "L'Islam de France sera-t-il républicain?"

19. Paul Bert, report to the Chamber of Deputies, May 31, 1888,

quoted in Alain Gresh, *L'Islam, la république et le monde* (Paris: Fayard, 2004), 185.

20. As Haarscher has pointed out, "In this context, the 'private' is not identified with individuality or inwardness, but with what is not political, while it may be 'social' (the economy, voluntary organizations, and so on)" (*La Laïcité*, 92).

21. The assistant to the mayor of Dreux in charge of school affairs declared that children who refused to eat meat would be expelled from cafeterias (Ahmed Taghza, "Des enfants musulmans refusent la viande non *hallal*," *L'Écho républicain*, November 25, 2004). Of course, the argument is that it's a question of "preventing nutritional deficiencies," which expulsion from the cafeteria would obviously remedy. The mayor of Dreux very quickly rejected his assistant's initiative.

22. Emmanuel Brenner, ed., *Les Territoires perdus de la république: Antisémitisme, racisme et sexisme en milieu scolaire* (Paris: Mille et Une Nuits, 2002).

2. Islam and Secularization

1. "The principle of tolerance and respect for freedom of conscience, thought, and religion [that] is a fundamental ethical position . . . cannot be reduced to placing on the same level the contents of different religious conceptions, as though an objective and universal truth no longer existed" (Cardinal Joseph Ratzinger, head of the Congregation for the Doctrine of the Faith, *Dominis Iesus*, Vatican, September 2000).

2. For an uncompromising expression of the refusal to see religion confined to the private sphere, see the speech delivered in New York to a commission of the General Assembly on item 105B, "Elimination of All Forms of Religious Intolerance," on October 26, 2004, by Monsignor Celestino Migliore, Vatican observer at the United Nations:

"The attitude of those who would like to confine religious expression to the private sphere alone ignores and denies the nature of authentic religious convictions. . . ." "The right of religious communities to express themselves in public" is unfortunately too often called into question, whereas "other social forces are authorized to do so." In addition, in recent times, the "juridical and legal approach to religious freedom" has tended more and more often "to drain it of its substance," he further stated. (*Le Jour du Seigneur*, France 2, November 7, 2004)

3. Marcel Gauchet, *The Disenchantment of the World*, trans. Oscar Burge (Princeton, N.J.: Princeton University Press, 1997). See also, for the legacy of Roman law and canon law, the works of Pierre Legendre.

4. I will confine myself to these arguments, aware that there are others finding Islam incompatible with the West because of jihad, anti-Semitism, the rejection of scientific analysis of the text of the Koran, and so on. But these arguments hardly hold water to the extent that they enjoy far from unanimous support among Muslims and because Christianity has, or has had, the same problems (think today of the campaign against Darwinism, shared by a segment of the American Christian Right and Islamic neofundamentalists).

5. The first form of acceptance of *laïcité* is thus to dissociate religion from any particular political system; continuing the comparison with Catholicism, this dissociation is explicit in the background of Cardinal Lavigerie's initiative, as reflected in the debate at the time (letter from Cardinal Rampolla to the bishop of Saint-Flour, where it is said that "the Church has nothing incompatible with any particular form of government" because "it is intent above all on the progress of religion, to the maintenance and growth of which it must endeavor to devote all its zeal and all its care" [Xavier de Montclos, *Le Toast d'Alger: Documents, 1890–1891* [Paris: De Boccard, 1965], 101). This goes without saying today, but it needed to be said at the time. This position would correspond today to that of many an ulema.

6. There is a clear presentation of these thinkers in Rachid Benzine, *Les Nouveaux Penseurs de l'Islam* (Paris: Albin Michel, 2004). See also Malek Chebel, *Manifeste pour un Islam des lumières: 27 propositions pour faire bouger l'Islam* (Paris: Hachette Littératures, 2004).

7. Soruch remains faithful here to a certain spirit of the Islamic revolution against the shah of Iran that Michel Foucault sensed: a religious revolution does not mean the advent of a better order but rather that it is impossible for temporal power to lay claim to absolute truth and transcendence. See Olivier Roy, "L'Énigme du soulèvement: Michel Foucault et l'Iran," *Vacarmes*, no. 28 (2004).

8. Rachid Benzine, interview in *La Croix*, February 13, 2004.

9. Olivier Roy, *Globalized Islam: The Search for a New Ummah* (New York: Columbia University Press, 2004).

10. Khaled Abu Fadl, "Striking a Balance: Islamic Legal Discourse on Muslim Minorities," in Yvonne Yazbek Haddad and John Esposito, eds., *Muslims on the Americanization Path?* (Atlanta: Scholars Press, 1998). He quotes in particular the fatwa by Rachid Ridha authorizing the Muslims of Bosnia-Herzegovina to remain in their country after it was annexed by Austria in 1908. Bernard Lewis expresses a divergent view in Bernard Lewis and Dominique Schnapper, eds., *Musulmans en Europe* (Aix-en-Provence: Actes Sud, 1992).

11. Olivier Carré, *L'Islam laïque; ou, Le retour à la grande tradition* (Paris: Armand Colin, 1993); Clifford Geertz, *Islam Observed* (New Haven, Conn.: Yale University Press, 1968). Conversely, a writer like Bernard Lewis, wishing to show the problems posed by Islam, treats only the Arab world, as in *The Crisis of Islam* (New York: Modern Library, 2003).

12. Carré, *L'Islam laïque*, 8.

13. Emmanuel Todd, *La Troisième Planète: Structures familiales et systèmes idéologiques* (Paris: Seuil, 1983).

14. I note in passing that predestination is called on to explain two contradictory attitudes: the supposed fatalism of the Arab (*mektoub* [it is written]) and the so-called entrepreneurial spirit of the Calvinist (looking in economic success for the sign of a salvation that will be known only on the Day of Judgment).

15. The U.S. military occupation of Iraq is based on this harsh pedagogy; the Coalition Provisional Authority in Iraq explicitly took the reconstruction of Germany after 1945 as its model: to teach the virtues of

democracy to a population brainwashed by despotism. The results do not seem conclusive.

16. This confusion is very clear in *Frère Tariq*, the book by Caroline Fourest on Tariq Ramadan, where she persists in describing him as a Muslim Brother, as though one were to call Allende a Communist or Jospin a Trotskyite. Indeed, what does the term "Muslim Brother" mean? Fidelity to a movement of thought; membership in an organization; the intent to institute a certain kind of state, a school of thought, a specific intellectual training, an ideological conviction? There are many ways of being or having been a Marxist, a Trotskyite, a follower of Action Française, or a fascist, and the same holds for the Muslim Brotherhood.

17. For Hizb ut-Tahrir, consult the Web site www.hizb-ut-tahrir.org.

18. Burcu Gültekin, *Instrumentalisation de l'Islam par une stratégie de promotion sociale à travers le secteur privé: Le cas du Müsiad* (Paris: Fondation Nationale des Sciences Politiques, 1999).

19. Olivier Roy, *The Failure of Political Islam*, trans. Carol Volk (Cambridge, Mass.: Harvard University Press, 1994).

20. Farhad Khosrokhavar and Olivier Roy, *Iran: Comment sortir d'une révolution religieuse* (Paris: Seuil, 1999).

3. The Crisis of the Secular State and the New Forms of Religiosity

1. Secularization had made itself felt in French society by the eighteenth century, but it was not until the 1940s that two chaplains raised an alarm that created a great stir in the Catholic hierarchy: Henri Godin and Yvan Daniel, *La France, pays de mission?* (Paris: Éditions de l'Abeille, 1943). They describe de-Christianization as a sociological fact, not the effect of political or philosophical propaganda.

2. For Christianity and sects, one may consult the works of Danièle Hervieu-Léger.

3. Olivier Roy, *Globalized Islam: The Search for a New Ummah* (New York: Columbia University Press, 2004).

4. We can, for example, refer to a number of cases that have not yet been well studied, such as the development of a Sufi Muslim sect established by European converts (the Mourabitounes) among the Indians of Chiapas in Mexico; conversions to Catholicism and Anglicanism in Turkey; the development of another Muslim brotherhood, the Haqqaniyya, in the United States; and so on.

5. David Landes, *Wealth and Poverty of Nations* (New York: Norton, 1998); Philip Bobbit, *The Shield of Achilles: War, Peace, and the Course of History* (New York: Knopf, 2002).

6. Marcel Gauchet examines the problem in the concluding chapters of *La Religion dans la démocratie: Parcours de la laïcité* (Paris: Gallimard, 1998).

7. Sébastien Fath, *Dieu bénisse l'Amérique* (Paris: Seuil, 2004).

8. Roy, *Globalized Islam.*

9. Tim Lahaye and Jerry B. Jenkins, *Left Behind: A Novel of the Earth's Last Days* (Wheaton, Ill.: Tyndale House, 1996). For some radical Muslims, the world is also on the road to ruin, except for a small minority, who are saved from hell.

10. Dominique Avon, "Une réponse à l'Islam 'réformiste' de Tariq Ramadan," *Nunc*, no. 4 (October 2003). Another equally open-minded critical point of view on Tariq Ramadan can be found in Sadri Khiari, "Tariq Ramadan, mythologie de la Umma et résistance culturelle," *Critique communiste*, March 2004.

11. "Any activity, however profane it may appear to be, that is nurtured by the remembrance of God, is holy: from daily hygiene to the sexual act, from prayer to fasting" (Tariq Ramadan, *Islam: Le face-à-face des civilisations* [Lyon: Tawhid, 1995], 321).

12. Jean-Hugues Roy reported:

The Superior Court in Montreal has given the Jewish community the right to install an *eruv*, a barely visible thread that enables them to avoid certain religious prohibitions on the sabbath. The Court invoked freedom of religion, but for other citizens of Outremont, this is a violation of the secular nature of Quebec society. . . . An *eruv* is a thread stretched between two buildings, which can be found, for example, on Fairmount Street in Montreal. It marks out, as it were, a territory that acts as an extension of the residence of Orthodox Jews. On the sabbath, the *eruv* allows them to use strollers or wheel chairs in public, something their religion normally prohibits. (Radio Canada, June 21, 2001)

13. I studied this development in *Globalized Islam*.

14. *Le Figaro*, November 27, 2004. On the different uses of the return to Islam made by young men and young women, see the excellent Nathalie Kakpo, "Jeunes issus de l'immigration et islam: Famille, école, travail et identifications religieuses" (Ph.D. diss., University of Paris VIII, 2004).

15. A meeting to set up a local branch of Ni putes ni soumises, held in the center of Dreux by two people who were not from the neighborhoods, was not attended by any girls from those neighborhoods. The organizer of the meeting explained it by the "weight of the community and the family," but a local reporter's investigation showed that the reasons for the lack of interest lay elsewhere: "This is not the *banlieue*"; "I don't believe I have to defend myself from being called a whore, because I'm not a whore"; "Me, I'm in favor of trying to find a consensus" (Pascal Boursier, "Ni putes, ni soumises ne mobilise pas," *L'Écho républicain*, May 12, 2004). You can see the disjunction between external global analyses that put religious traditions in the forefront and the lived experience, which consists of action rather than submission, of the girls who were interviewed.

16. Farhad Khosrokhavar, *L'Islam des jeunes* (Paris: Flammarion, 1997).

4. De Facto Secularization

1. Olivier Roy, *The Failure of Political Islam*, trans. Carol Volk (Cambridge: Harvard University Press, 1994).

2. Clearly, the new generation of Front National militants no longer considers the fight against abortion an essential cause, whereas the old guard has held on to very conservative positions.

INDEX